CAMPFIRE
CUISINE

Library of Congress Cataloging
in Publication Number: 2005932398

ISBN: 1-59474-085-2

Printed in Singapore
Typeset in Mrs. Eaves
Designed by Bryn Ashburn
Illustrations by Dushan Milic

Distributed in North America
by Chronicle Books
85 Second Street
San Francisco, CA 94105

10 9 8 7 6 5 4 3 2 1

Quirk Books
215 Church Street
Philadelphia, PA 19106
www.quirkbooks.com

CAMPFIRE CUISINE

GOURMET RECIPES FOR THE GREAT OUTDOORS

by Robin Donovan

QUIRK BOOKS

PHILADELPHIA

Table of Contents

Introduction

Tent? Check. Sleeping bag? Check. Mosquito repellent? Check. Extra-virgin olive oil? Check.

Huh?

Every spring, as throngs of outdoor adventurers ready their camping gear and ponder whether to head for the mountains or the desert, the coast or the woods, all I can think about is dinner.

Don't get me wrong. I love the outdoors as much as the next guy. But I have to admit that for me the highlight of any camping trip is the food. Meals around the campfire are the pinnacle of my camping experience.

"Food snob," my friends sneer, rolling their eyes, as I nix their dinner suggestions of canned franks and beans. Many of my friends, I've discovered, are among the majority of campers, who—while waxing rhapsodic about the pleasures of sleeping outdoors, breathing clean air, and communing with nature—have resigned themselves to eating unhealthy, unsatisfying foods in order to enjoy the great outdoors.

"It never occurred to me that you could cook anything really good at a campsite," my friend Susan said to me recently. Susan swears that she and her husband ate macaroni and cheese out of a box every single night of a recent three-week camping trip.

Other friends share grisly tales starring soggy concoctions of canned meats and rehydrated vegetables, strange combinations of processed foods congealing on plastic plates, dishes with scary names like "Ramen Cheeseburger Soup" or "Cottage Cheese Cabbage Noodles." How these people can stomach something called "Can Can Quickie"—which, by the way, contains a can of something identified mysteriously as "luncheon meat"—is beyond me.

It's not that my friends don't appreciate a good meal. In fact, many of them are quite the foodies back home, in the convenience of their well-stocked, professionally equipped kitchens. A few are even considered geniuses of backyard barbecue. But drop them thirty miles from the nearest grocery store with a couple of pans, some aluminum foil, a camp stove, and a fire pit, and suddenly they're like helpless kittens crying for a bowl of milk. "We're hungry," they whine. "Where are the hot dogs?"

But I have always subscribed to the "live to eat" philosophy of life—and of vacationing. After all, isn't pleasure the whole point of a vacation? And isn't eating delicious foods one of the greatest pleasures of all? More often than not, I've chosen travel destinations based on the menu offerings. Dreams of rich cheeses and flaky pastries propelled me to France. The promise of delicate pastas, chewy breads, and salty cured meats lured me to Italy. I ventured to Thailand for pungent peanut sauce and fiery coconut curry. My memories of Indonesia are animated by a parade of pancakes drizzled with palm sugar syrup, bowls of rich yellow rice, and platters of pork braised in sweet soy sauce. If my penchant for tasty food could so easily tempt me to travel all the way around the world, you can bet I'm not going to go tromping out into the California wilderness without something scrumptious to look forward to. So for many years, I simply avoided camping altogether. The "reward" just didn't seem worth the effort.

Then one summer some friends dragged me on a camping trip to Pinnacles National Monument, a jumble of craggy peaks and natural caves bordering California's arid Salinas Valley. "It'll be fun," they promised. "It's really beautiful. You'll like it." I remained skeptical. But I nonetheless packed my borrowed camping equipment, put on a brave face, and squeezed into the car.

We arrived at the campsite just before dusk and quickly set up our tents before it became too dark to see what we were doing. Once my sleeping arrangements were squared away, I wondered, "Now what? It's too early to go to bed, but what the hell else are we going to do?"

I ventured out of my tent to find my friend Heida expertly building a fire. Sean was sitting at the picnic table, busily cutting vegetables. Piles of chopped onions, mushrooms, and brightly colored bell peppers grew in front of him. Then from the cooler he pulled out a container full of chunks of marinated chicken. I sat down with him, and we began threading the chicken and chopped vegetables onto bamboo skewers. Heida and the others joined us, one by one, until all of us were kebabing away. In no time, the piles of meat and vegetables were transformed into an artful stack of kebabs. Someone sliced some potatoes and onions; tossed them with olive oil, Dijon mustard, and fresh herbs; and bundled them into squares of aluminum foil.

Soon the foil packets hissed on the grill. The kebabs sizzled as their juices trickled into the fire. We all gathered around expectantly, poking at the fire with long sticks, sipping red wine from coffee mugs, breathing in the smells of wood smoke, browning meat, and herbs wafting up from the glowing pit.

Finally, dinner was served, and I can say in all honesty that it was one of the best meals I've ever had. There is just something about a meal that is prepared and consumed in the fresh air, under the twinkling stars, far from the bustle of everyday life, using only the most basic tools. Meat tastes meatier, herbs brighter, vegetables earthier. My stomach happily sated, I slept a deep sleep that night, bundled in my cozy sleeping bag, cradled by the sounds of the outdoors.

Pinnacles is, in fact, a stunningly beautiful spot. The next morning, after a breakfast of scrambled eggs and home fries made from the packets of leftover potatoes from the night before, we set out on a long hike up the rocky trail, through the dark, damp caves, to the highest sun-baked peak. After a twelve-mile hike in blazing heat, we returned to camp with new appetites. More treats were pulled from coolers, and collective effort yielded another satisfying meal. That night, as I lay in my tent listening to the crackle of twigs made by wild pigs rooting in the woods around our campsite, I fully embraced my inner nature lover. If this was camping, I was all for it. I realized that the reward is, in fact, well worth the effort.

Since then I've camped—and cooked—at dozens of sites throughout the West. I've made bourbon-glazed chicken in the mountains, grilled steak tacos in the desert, and pan-seared tequila shrimp on the coast. More often than not, while my companions are debating where to go and what to do, I'm already busy planning the menu.

What I've learned is that outdoor cooking doesn't need to be elaborate in order to yield stunning results. As I've discovered, the mantra of many a renowned chef has never been more appropriate: Good food, simply prepared, tastes good. Armed with quality ingredients and the recipes and advice in this book, even the staunchest gourmet will finally feel safe venturing out into the wild. Mother Nature kindly provides ambience any fine restaurant would kill for: Stars twinkle overhead, the flickering fire casts a romantic glow, and a cool summer breeze makes subtle background music. All you need to add is a well-stocked cooler, a few essential pieces of equipment, and a well-thought-out meal plan, and you, too, can create top-notch meals around a campfire.

Your friends may resist your gourmet tendencies at first. But I guarantee that when dinnertime rolls around, snide comments will be silenced by the hungry crowd thoroughly enjoying the food. In the end, everyone will appreciate having a foodie along.

PART I

RECIPE FOR A DELICIOUS, GOURMET CAMPING TRIP

GEAR UP: EVERYTHING YOU NEED

You may feel overwhelmed at the thought of equipping a gourmet camping kitchen, but you'll be surprised at how easy it is. You probably have most of the items you'll need, and those you don't are easy to find. Stock your portable camp kitchen with a few essentials, and you'll be able to cook almost anything in the wild that you cook at home.

You can pack lightly if you plan dishes that use the same preparation methods and cookware over the course of your trip. All the recipes in this book can be cooked either directly on a grill, wrapped in foil on a grill, or in a 2-quart pot or 10-inch skillet on a simple camp stove. (Use these sizes for the recipes unless otherwise noted.)

A modest supply of kitchen equipment will be more than sufficient for just about any camp cooking. Scour tag sales, flea markets, and thrift stores for inexpensive cookware and utensils. Purchase a couple of large plastic storage bins to contain everything you need for a camp kitchen that's ready to go whenever the urge strikes.

MUST-HAVE EQUIPMENT

Cooler
Plastic cutting board
Sharp knife
Cheese grater (ideally, one with small holes to double as a citrus zester)
Vegetable peeler (doubles as a cheese slicer)
Can/bottle opener
Measuring cups
Measuring spoons
Tongs
Spatula
10-inch skillet with lid (preferably nonstick)
2-quart pot with lid
Camp stove and fuel
Plates
Mugs
Spoons, forks, and knives
Lantern
Sponge
Scrubber

MUST-HAVE SUPPLIES

Aluminum foil
Ziplock bags
Dish soap (biodegradable)
Charcoal briquettes
Lighter fluid or a chimney starter (unless you're using fast-lighting briquettes)
Firewood
Matches (waterproof/"strike anywhere")
Wooden skewers
Plastic garbage bags
Paper towels

A FEW ITEMS THAT ARE REALLY NICE TO HAVE BUT NOT ESSENTIAL

Headlamp (great for cooking or doing dishes after dark!)
Plastic coffee-filter cone and paper coffee filters, or a French press (if you're coffee drinkers)
Corkscrew (a must if you plan to have wine on your trip)
Garlic press
Grilling basket for fish or seafood
Grill rack (place it on top of an existing grill, or use it to create your own barbecue)
Kitchen shears
Insulated lunch bag

CHOOSING THE CAMP STOVE THAT'S RIGHT FOR YOU

There are dozens of good camping stoves on the market—ranging in price from as low as $20 to $200 or more—and virtually any one of them is suitable for the recipes in this book. Although plenty of fancier options are available, even the simplest stove—nothing more than a burner that screws onto a propane canister—will be sufficient for all the recipes in this book.

So how do you choose which stove is right for you? Three simple questions should help you narrow the choices:

1. **How many people will you be cooking for, and what types of meals will you be cooking?** Knowing how many people you'll be serving and how complex the meals will be will help you determine what size stove you need. If you're cooking only simple meals for yourself or for yourself and one other person, a single-burner stove is probably sufficient. If you'll regularly be cooking more elaborate meals or cooking for a crowd, you may want to look into larger, multiburner options.

2. **What's the weather going to be like?** If you'll be cooking only in temperate weather, just about any stove will do. A stove with windscreens is good in the event of windy conditions.

   Temperature also affects your choice of fuel. For instance, a butane-fueled stove will work only in temperatures of 32°F or above. Pure propane will work down to 0°F. White gas can be used in just about any weather conditions.

   Choice of fuel may also be influenced by where you plan to travel. Kerosene, for instance, is widely available throughout the world, while butane and white gas are difficult to find outside the United States and Canada.

OTHER THINGS TO CONSIDER WHEN CHOOSING A STOVE

- How easy is the stove to set up?
- How sturdy is it?
- How easy is the stove to light?
- How easily is the heat output adjusted?
- Does the stove require elaborate maintenance (either on the trail or between trips)?

3. **What types of trips will you be taking with your stove?** Camp stoves come in a vast array of sizes, from teeny, tiny lightweight backpacking "microstoves" to massive platforms that would serve an army platoon. For most trips, something in the middle will suffice. While a backpacking stove might be too small to heat a 10- or 12-inch skillet properly, the super monster models practically require a truck to haul them around.

   If you'll need to carry your stove a significant distance from your car to your campsite, or if you'll be cooking for only two people, stick with a single-burner version. If you plan to use the stove only for car camping or to cook for larger groups, a more robust model may be in order. You should choose the smallest, lightest stove that will suit your needs.

PLAY IT SAFE: STORING, TRANSPORTING, AND PREPARING FOOD SAFELY

Contrary to popular belief, food poisoning is not just an excuse to play hooky from work. It is very real, and it's certainly not something you'll want to deal with in the wild. Proper storage, handling, and preparation of food can protect you from this unpleasant, potentially dangerous malady.

BUYING AND STORING FOOD

- When buying fresh meat, poultry, or seafood, always check the "sell by" and "use by" dates. Do not purchase or use these or other foods once these dates have passed.
- When storing meat, poultry, or seafood in a cooler, be sure to wrap the packages in multiple layers of plastic or foil to prevent leaks.
- Always refrigerate perishable foods within 2 hours of purchasing (within 1 hour if the room or outside temperature is above 90°F).
- Store canned food in a cool, clean, dry place.
- Discard any cans of food that are dented, leaking, bulging, or rusted.
- If you are camping in an area where bears may be present, store food in airtight containers in bear lockers, bear canisters, the trunk of your vehicle, or suspended from a tree (at least 15 feet high, 4 feet from the tree trunk, and 100 yards from your campsite).

PACK YOUR COOLER THE RIGHT WAY

Follow these tips to keep your food cool and safe.

- Use an appliance thermometer to be sure your cooler stays at 40°F or below (frozen foods you want to keep frozen should be stored at 0°F or below).
- Prechill your cooler by filling it with ice 30 minutes before adding food.
- Prechill all food and beverages before adding to the cooler.
- Prefreeze meat, poultry, seafood, fruit, and noncarbonated beverages—already frozen, they'll help your cooler stay cold longer.
- Bags of frozen vegetables (such as corn and peas) double as ice packs, helping to keep the cooler cold until you're ready to defrost or cook them.
- Block ice will last longer than ice cubes or ice chunks. Make your own block ice by freezing water-filled 1-gallon or 1/2-gallon resealable freezer bags. (Use the type of freezer bags that stand up on their own for easy filling.) To minimize leakage as the ice melts, double-bag the ice blocks.
- Pack the food you will use first on top, and try to group the food by meal to avoid unnecessary opening and rearranging of the cooler.
- Keep nonperishable beverages in one cooler, perishable food and beverages in another.

- Keep the coolers well stocked with ice, and open them as little as possible.
- Keep the coolers in a shady spot or in the coolest part of your car.
- If you're planning a long trip, split your food in two. Fill one cooler with what you need for the first half of the trip. (Plan to eat the most perishable items in the first half of the trip.) Place food you won't need until the second half of the trip in a second cooler, pack it with ice, and seal it with duct tape. Don't open it until it's time to start using that food.

SAFE STORAGE TIMES FOR PERISHABLES

The chart below lists safe storage times for perishable foods in a cooler kept at 40°F or below. Frozen foods stored at 0°F or below will last much longer. But since it is difficult to keep foods frozen in a cooler, it's best to use these time guidelines even if the food starts out frozen at the beginning of your trip. Use an appliance thermometer to be sure your cooler stays at 40°F or below.

Eggs (fresh, raw, in shell)	3 weeks
Eggs (hard-boiled)	1 week
Liquid pasteurized egg substitutes (opened)	3 days
Liquid pasteurized egg substitutes (unopened)	10 days
Mayonnaise	2 months
Steaks, chops, and roasts (raw)	3 to 5 days
Ground meat (raw beef, turkey, veal, pork, or lamb)	1 to 2 days
Chicken (uncooked; whole or in pieces)	1 to 2 days
Fish and seafood (raw)	1 to 2 days
Homemade egg salad, chicken salad, or tuna salad	3 to 5 days
Hot dogs (opened package)	1 week
Hot dogs (unopened package)	2 weeks
Cold cuts (opened package)	3 to 5 days
Cold cuts (unopened package)	2 weeks
Bacon	1 week
Sausage (raw; made from chicken, turkey, pork, or beef)	1 to 2 days
Sausage (smoked)	1 week

Note: Storage times recommended by the U.S. Department of Agriculture.

PREPARING FOOD SAFELY

- Always wash your hands thoroughly with antibacterial soap before and after handling food.
- Keep raw meat, poultry, and seafood away from other food.
- Keep raw meat, poultry, and seafood in the cooler until they're ready to cook.
- Always thaw frozen meat, poultry, or seafood thoroughly before cooking to ensure that it cooks evenly.
- Frozen foods should be thawed in a cooler at 40°F or below. Be sure thawing meat, poultry, or seafood is well wrapped to avoid dripping juices onto other food.
- To thaw food more quickly, place it in a sealed, leak-proof plastic bag, and submerge the bag in cold water. Change the water every 30 minutes until the food is completely thawed. Cook immediately.
- Never use the same dishes or utensils for both raw and cooked meat, poultry, or seafood.
- After cutting raw meat, wash your hands and the cutting board, knife, and work surfaces with hot, soapy water.
- Always keep marinating meat in a cooler with a temperature of 40°F or below.

If you're unsure how to tell when meat is fully cooked, use a meat thermometer. Insert it into the thickest part of the meat to test for the proper temperature:

Ground meat (beef, veal, lamb, and pork)	160°F (at least)
Ground poultry	165°F
Beef, veal, and lamb (steaks, chops, or roasts)	145°F
Pork (chops or roasts)	160°F
Dark poultry meat	180°F
Poultry breast meat	170°F

Note: Temperatures recommended by the USDA.

CHAPTER 3
GET READY TO COOK

It's been thousands of years since our species figured out how to make fire, yet in this modern age, fire making is a skill few of us possess. I have spent many a frustrating hour hunched over a smoldering fire pit, breathing in a sad stream of smoke from a flameless pile of sticks and paper. But building a fire doesn't have to be a frustrating endeavor. Just follow the simple steps here, and soon you'll be enjoying the cozy warmth and glow of your very own campfire.

TURN UP THE HEAT

Before beginning, check the regulations in the area you are visiting to be sure that fires are allowed and to determine whether they must be built only in designated areas such as fire pits. Restrictions can be seasonal, depending on the fire hazard from dry vegetation, so even a place where fires were permitted on your last trip may not allow them now. Also check on regulations regarding the gathering of firewood and kindling. Many parks and recreation areas forbid gathering, in which case you'll need to come prepared with your own firewood and kindling. Often the campground host will sell firewood. It costs a bit more than if you bought it before leaving home, but the convenience can't be beat.

A FEW WORDS OF CAUTION

Forest fires are a real threat—both to the environment and to those enjoying the wilderness—so always use caution when building fires in the outdoors. Here are a few things to remember:

- Always be sure an adult is attending the fire; never leave a fire unattended.
- Warn young children to stay away from the fire pit. Rocks, grates, and fire-pit walls can get extremely hot, so children should be kept a good distance from the fire and fire pit at all times, even when the fire is dead (hot coals can remain under ashes that look cold).
- Do not place flammable items (shoes, towels, paper plates, lighter fluid, etc.) on or near the edge of the fire pit.
- Never build a fire within 10 feet of tents, camp stoves or fuel canisters, or sleeping areas containing flammable materials. Do not build a fire below low-hanging branches.
- Always be sure the fire is fully extinguished before leaving the area or going to bed. To extinguish a campfire, stir the coals and ashes with a long stick to spread them out and expose their surfaces to the air; then slowly pour water over the coals, keeping your face and hands away from the rising steam, until the fire is completely extinguished ("dead out" in ranger parlance).

You'll need:

- Sticks, twigs, or other kindling material
- Newspaper, cardboard, or other easy-to-ignite paper products
- Several dry logs of varying thickness, in lengths to fit within your fire pit or containment area
- Wooden matches, preferably waterproof and "strike anywhere"

Many campsites have prebuilt fire pits. If the site you're visiting doesn't have one, check that new pits are permitted. If so, choose a spot at least 10 feet from tents, trees, or other flammable items, and check to be sure that there are no low-hanging branches overhead. Clear an area about 3 feet in diameter and enclose it with a ring of rocks just inside the perimeter of the cleared circle.

Build a pyramid of twigs in your designated fire pit to start your fire.

Now that you've got your firewood, kindling, and a fire pit, you're ready to build your fire.

1. Make a small pile of twigs and paper scraps in the middle of your fire pit.
2. Over the twig pile, construct a "teepee" of small sticks, balancing the sticks against each other so that they stand in the teepee shape with room for air to circulate underneath.
3. Light a match and hold it to the twigs and paper scraps until they ignite. Light the kindling in several places.
4. When the sticks catch fire, begin adding pieces of wood that gradually increase in size, waiting for them to catch fire before adding the larger pieces.
5. Once you've got a good, strong fire, add increasingly thicker logs. Be sure to lean them against each other, always leaving room for air to circulate underneath.

Choose Your Cooking Methods

Before setting out on your wilderness adventure, you'll need to do a bit of planning. A crucial part of this planning lies in researching what types of facilities will be available to you. Will you have a fire pit at your campsite? A grill? Or will you be doing all your cooking on a camp stove?

Once you've determined what cooking facilities will be available, you can plan your menus, which will inform your choice of specific cooking equipment and staples. Below I offer basic tips and guidelines for the three outdoor cooking methods you'll use the most: cooking on a grill, cooking in foil, and cooking on a camp stove. Each section includes information on special tools or equipment you'll need for that cooking method. In addition, be sure to read the chapter "Gear Up: Everything You Need" (page 14) to learn about the necessities for successful campsite cooking.

READY, SET, GRILL!

Grilling food over hot coals is one of the most satisfying cooking methods—you hear the food sizzling, smell the earthy aroma of flame-licked meat and veggies, see the grill marks appearing as the food caramelizes before your eyes. Plus it's a fast way to cook delicious meals without a big mess to clean up.

Wood Coals or Charcoal Briquettes?

Wood is an appealing cooking fuel to many because it doesn't require lighter fluid, which is damaging to the environment, and wood smoke adds a nice flavor to the food being grilled. Just about any type of wood can be used, provided it is dry and not resinous. Hardwoods such as chicory, oak, and maple are the most popular for grilling. The main drawback of using wood for cooking is that it takes a long time for the logs to burn into a glowing bed of coals, but the resulting flavor is worth the wait.

Charcoal briquettes, which can be purchased in any supermarket, are more widely available and easier to transport, and many campers find them more convenient for cooking than wood. Fast-lighting and "light-in-bag" varieties come presoaked with lighter fluid, making them even more convenient. A "chimney starter" also makes lighting charcoal briquettes effortless, and you won't need lighter fluid at all.

What You'll Need

- A fire pit or freestanding barbecue. (Many campsites have fire pits and many also have barbecues. If yours doesn't, see page 24 for tips on creating a fire pit from scratch.)
- A metal grill or grate. (Many fire pits or built-in barbecues have grills, but for cleanliness, you may prefer to bring your own to lay on top of or above what's there. Just about any metal rack will work—take the grill from your home barbecue, or even an oven rack. You can create a makeshift grill by building a fire pit and balancing a grill rack between the stones of your fire ring.)
- Firewood and kindling, or charcoal and lighter fluid (unless you're using fast-lighting charcoal or a chimney starter)
- Matches (wooden, preferably waterproof and "strike anywhere")
- Long-handled metal spatula
- Tongs

Preparing Wood Coals

If you're planning to use wood coals, follow the directions in the section on lighting a fire (see page 24). Bear in mind that you won't need a huge fire for cooking. An overly large fire not only poses an increased fire hazard, but it will also require more time to burn down into usable coals, so keep it on the small side. Once you've got a good, blazing fire going, let it burn at least 45 minutes, or until you have a bed of red, glowing coals ready for grilling. Using a poker or long stick, spread out the coals.

Preparing Charcoal Briquettes

- Using a Chimney Starter: The most environmentally sensitive way to light charcoal briquettes is to use a "chimney starter"—a cylindrical device designed for the lighting of briquettes without the use of lighter fluid. If you've brought one, place it in your fire pit or on your grill's charcoal grate. Stuff some wadded newspaper into the bottom section. Fill the top section with briquettes. Light the newspaper and, if necessary, fan the opening to help the briquettes ignite. Once the coals have ignited, it can take from 15 to 30 minutes before they are ready to use. Once the flames begin to lick the briquettes at the top of the starter and a white ash covers most of the coals, carefully tip the starter, pouring the coals into the fire pit or onto the charcoal grate. Spread out the coals, using a long stick or poker.

- Using Briquettes with Lighter Fluid: Pile the briquettes in the center of your fire pit or the charcoal grate of a barbecue. Douse with lighter fluid, and let it soak in for 3 to 4 minutes. Light the briquettes in several places. They will need to burn for 30 to 40 minutes before they are ready for grilling. You'll know the briquettes are ready when they are glowing red and are mostly covered with white ash. When they have reached this point, spread them out in your cooking area.

- Using Fast-Lighting or "Light-in-Bag" Briquettes: These easy-to-use briquettes come presoaked with lighter fluid. Simply pile them in the middle of your fire pit or on the charcoal grate of your barbecue, and light with a match. If you are using "light-in-bag" briquettes, place the whole, unopened bag in the middle of the fire pit or on the grate of the barbecue, and light the bag itself. The briquettes will need to burn for 30 to 40 minutes before they are ready for grilling. When they are glowing and are mostly covered with white ash, spread out the briquettes in your cooking area.

Measuring the Heat of Your Fire

Probably the biggest challenge for the campfire cook is getting the heat of the fire just right for cooking. If the heat isn't right, your dish—no matter how good your recipe or ingredients—can be ruined. This simple technique for judging the heat beforehand will help to prevent culinary disasters caused by trying to cook over a too-hot or too-cool fire.

To determine how hot a fire is, place your hand just above the grill and count seconds. When a fire is hot ("high heat"), you'll need to pull your hand away in 1 to 2 seconds. With a medium fire ("medium heat"), you'll be able to keep your hand there for about 3 seconds. With a "slow" fire ("low heat"), you can keep your hand there for 4 to 5 seconds. This method also works for stove-top cooking.

Creating Distinct "Cooking Zones"

Once your coals are ready for cooking, you can create "cooking zones" by varying the depth of coals in different areas under the grill. The closer the coals are to the grill, the higher the heat will be in that area. By creating different temperature zones, you can simultaneously cook foods requiring different heat levels.

Create three distinct cooking zones by dividing the grilling area into three sections. For high heat, layer the briquettes under one section so they are just 4 to 6 inches from the grill rack. For medium heat, pile the briquettes under the second section so there are 8 to 10 inches of space between them and the grill. For low heat in the third section, spread the coals so there is a 12-inch space between the coals and the grill.

Pile the coals in three distinct heat zones.

WRAP IT UP: COOKING IN FOIL

Cooking foil-wrapped food over hot coals is a convenient way to create dishes with multiple ingredients and complex flavors. The important things to remember are to use a heavy-duty foil (to avoid breakage) and to leave room inside the foil (to allow heat and steam to circulate). You are essentially creating a mini oven in which to bake your food.

Cooking in foil is an ideal preparation method for fish too delicate to keep from flaking apart on a grill rack or for dishes in which you want to retain the sauce and juices as they cook.

Foil can also be used to protect food you wish to cook directly in the coals. Whole potatoes and yams wrapped in foil, for example, can be baked in the glowing coals (this is one instance where you don't need to leave room inside the packet). Cook the yams or potatoes about 45 minutes, or until they are easily punctured with a skewer.

For the recipes in this book that use the foil-baking method, use fairly large squares of foil—about 12 inches by 12 inches. This will allow enough room for the specified quantity of food to fit with space left for heat and steam to circulate inside the foil packet.

To prevent food sticking to the foil, always coat it with oil or butter before adding the food. I prefer to use olive oil spray for most dishes, as it contributes flavor as well as nonstick qualities, but any nonstick cooking-oil spray will do. Alternatively, use a paper towel to rub 1/2 teaspoon or so of olive oil, vegetable oil, or butter on the foil.

Cooking in foil has other advantages, too: Packets can be made up ahead of time and stored in a cooler until ready to cook, leftovers can be kept in their cooking packets for storage, and cleanup couldn't be easier.

TOP IT OFF: COOKING ON A CAMP STOVE

For everything from boiling water for your morning coffee to cooking rice or stir-fries, a camp stove is a necessity. Using a camp stove is the simplest way to cook at a campsite, as it doesn't require building a fire or waiting for coals to burn down. Simply turn on the stove, light it, and you're ready to start cooking.

You can cook anything on a camp stove that you can cook on your stove top at home—and the methods are the same as for cooking on a gas burner in your kitchen. The only limiting factors are your available ingredients and the cookware you've brought along.

Use the method described above ("Measuring the Heat of Your Fire," page 26) to determine the heat of your pans on the stove. Adjust the flame accordingly.

See the chapter "Gear Up: Everything You Need" (page 14) for information on how to choose the camp stove that's right for you.

IS IT DONE YET?

Below are general guidelines for cooking seafood, poultry and other meat, vegetables, and fruit on the grill. Times will vary based on the thickness and density of your meat as well as on the wide variations between grills, the distance between the heat source and the grill rack, and even the weather. The times given below are based on an average of these factors, so you should adjust your times accordingly.

Note that, after cooking, larger cuts of meat should always be allowed to rest, covered loosely with foil, for at least 5 minutes before cutting. This allows the meat to reabsorb its juices. Keep in mind that the meat will continue to cook a bit during this time, so you should take it off the heat just before it reaches your desired doneness.

Beef

Burgers (1½ inches thick)	rare: 3 to 4 minutes per side
	medium: 5 to 6 minutes per side
	well-done: 6 to 7 minutes per side
Steaks (1 inch thick)	rare: 3 to 4 minutes per side
	medium: 5 to 6 minutes per side
	well-done: 6 to 7 minutes per side
Larger cuts (such as tri-tip)	15 to 20 minutes per pound, turning regularly
Beef skewers	5 to 10 minutes, turning regularly

Fish and Shellfish

As a general rule, allow 7 to 8 minutes per inch of thickness.

Fillets (½ inch thick)	2 to 3 minutes per side
Fillets (½ inch thick), wrapped in foil	8 to 10 minutes
Fillets (1 inch thick), wrapped in foil	15 to 20 minutes
Fish steaks (1 inch thick)	3 to 5 minutes per side
Whole small fish (such as trout)	5 to 6 minutes per side
Whole large fish (3+ pounds)	15 minutes per side
Large prawns	3 to 4 minutes per side
Sea scallops	2 to 3 minutes per side
Prawns, scallops, squid, wrapped in foil	15 to 20 minutes
Mussels, clams, oysters	5 minutes
Mussels, clams, oysters, wrapped in foil	8 to 10 minutes

Lamb

Loin chops (1 inch thick, bone in)	rare: 3 to 4 minutes per side
	medium: 5 to 6 minutes per side
	well-done: 7 to 8 minutes per side
Loin chops (3 inch thick, bone in)	rare: 6 to 8 minutes per side
	medium: 8 to 10 minutes per side
	well-done: 10 to 12 minutes per side
Lamb skewers	10 to 15 minutes, turning regularly

Pork

Boneless chops (¾ inch thick)	7 to 8 minutes per side
Loin chop (1 inch thick)	8 to 10 minutes per side
Pork loin roast	about 20 minutes per pound, turning regularly
Pork skewers	10 to 12 minutes, turning regularly

Poultry

Chicken breasts (bone in)	12 to 15 minutes per side
Chicken breasts (boneless)	7 to 8 minutes per side
Chicken drumsticks, thighs, wings (bone in)	7 to 8 minutes per side
Chicken thighs (boneless)	4 to 5 minutes per side
Chicken skewers	10 minutes, turning regularly
Duck breast (boneless, skinless)	8 to 10 minutes per side

Vegetables

Corn, whole cob, cooked in foil or husk	10 to 15 minutes
Eggplant	5 to 6 minutes per side
Mushrooms, on skewers	5 minutes per side
Mushrooms, wrapped in foil	15 to 20 minutes
Onions, on skewers	5 minutes per side
Onions, whole, wrapped in foil	25 to 30 minutes
Peppers	5 minutes per side
Potatoes, whole, wrapped in foil	45 to 50 minutes
Potatoes, sliced, wrapped in foil	30 to 35 minutes
Tomatoes, halved, wrapped in foil	10 to 15 minutes

Fruit

Apples, sliced, cooked in foil	10 to 15 minutes
Bananas, cooked in peel, wrapped in foil	10 to 15 minutes
Peaches, apricots, halved, wrapped in foil	10 to 15 minutes

CHAPTER 4
FOCUS ON FLAVOR: STOCKING YOUR PANTRY

When you are working with a limited number of ingredients, a focus on flavor is essential. Herbs, spices, and strongly flavored condiments can completely transform the character of a dish. A strong cheese—such as crumbled feta or grated Parmesan—does wonders for a simple salad. Rosemary adds complexity to a basic chicken marinade. Cured olives give sauces and salads an unexpected depth of flavor. And, as any foodie knows, good olive oil is a must.

Enhancing Flavor

There are countless simple ways to enhance flavor. Here are just a few:

- Marinating meats anywhere from 1 hour to overnight both adds flavor and tenderizes the meat. Mix the marinade in a large ziplock bag, add the meat, seal, and store in a cooler until ready to cook.
- Brining meat—marinating it in a mixture of water, salt, sugar, and spices for anywhere from a few hours to several days—renders it extremely tender. This method is especially suited to pork, which can be dry and flavorless if not prepared well.
- Citrus zest (lemon, lime, or orange) adds intense flavor to marinades and salad dressings.
- Fresh herbs—basil, mint, thyme, rosemary, oregano, cilantro, and so on—add a bright, fresh element to marinades, sauces, and salads.
- Compound butters—butters that have been softened and combined with herbs and spices—are a cinch to make at home and are great melted on grilled meats and vegetables or spread on a split and toasted loaf of French bread. See the recipes on pages 60 to 62 for several versions. Form these mixtures into logs wrapped in plastic wrap, and refrigerate or freeze until ready to use. Slice off bits as needed.
- Flavored oils—from roasted garlic to black truffle—can be added to sauces or simply drizzled over grilled meat, vegetables, or pasta. You'll find a wide array of these in specialty food stores or the gourmet food section of your supermarket.
- Flavored vinegars—raspberry, fig, tarragon, and so on—can be mixed with olive oil to make flavorful dressings and marinades. These can be found in specialty food stores or the gourmet food section of your supermarket.
- Hot sauces, chiles, and salsas spice up any dish that needs a little extra kick.
- Strong cheeses, olives, and nuts add complexity to salads and cooked dishes—and they do double duty as healthy snacks.

PANTRY STAPLES

Camping supply stores sell miniature spice racks, or you can use any small jars or plastic containers. Pack staples in clearly labeled plastic storage bins.

Below is a list of basic items you should always make sure to have in your camping pantry.

Spices
Salt (kosher salt is additive-free and has the cleanest flavor)
Pepper
Cayenne

Herbs
Dried and/or fresh oregano
Dried and/or fresh thyme
Dried and/or fresh basil
Dried and/or fresh rosemary

Cooking Fats
Olive oil
Olive oil spray and/or nonstick cooking spray
Butter

Produce
Onions and/or shallots
Garlic
Lemons, limes, and oranges

Canned Goods
Chicken or vegetable broth
Diced tomatoes
Vinegar (balsamic, wine, sherry, etc.)
Soy sauce
Mayonnaise
Mustard (Dijon, whole grain, honey, etc.)
Ketchup
Salsa

Sweet Stuff
Honey
Maple syrup
White sugar
Brown sugar

MAKE-AHEAD STAPLES

I've designed the recipes in this book to be simple enough to cook at a campsite, though many of them—especially sauces, dressings, marinades, spice rubs, and other condiments—can be made at home ahead of time to save you the trouble of bringing along all the individual ingredients. I've included notes with such recipes indicating that they can be made ahead and offering storage instructions where necessary.

The one recipe I highly recommend making at home in a large batch is Multipurpose Baking Mix (see recipe below). This versatile baking mix is the basis of pancakes, dumplings, scones, and biscuits (see recipes, pages 67, 134, 70, and 179). While you could make this at a campsite, lugging along a big bag of flour—plus baking powder and baking soda—just seems impractical. Also, unlike most cooking, baking is an exact science, and precise measuring is simply easier to accomplish in your home kitchen.

Multipurpose Baking Mix

Make a triple or quadruple batch of this recipe, divide it into 1- or 2-cup portions, and store it in ziplock bags in a dry place until ready to use.

> 2 cups all-purpose flour
> 2 teaspoons baking powder
> 1 teaspoon baking soda
> 1 teaspoon salt
> 1 teaspoon sugar

Mix all the ingredients until well combined.

CHAPTER 5

MENU PLANNING

Once you've nailed down the basic details of where you'll go and how long you'll stay, you'll want to map out a meal plan; create a menu for each breakfast, lunch, and dinner; and build your shopping list.

When planning meals, it's important to consider how long different foods will last in a cooler. Fish, for instance, shouldn't be kept for more than a day or two, while steak (properly stored) will be fine for several days. Likewise, lettuce begins to wilt after a day or two, but heartier vegetables such as asparagus, cauliflower, and zucchini can last up to a week or longer. Cheese, tofu, and pre-cooked meats such as smoked sausages are great for meals later in the trip, as they will last a week or longer in a cooler that's regularly restocked with ice. Canned beans will last forever, and with the addition of fresh vegetables and spices, they make an excellent one-pot meal. Plan to cook the most perishable items first and the longer-lasting items last. Refer to the chapter "Play It Safe: Storing, Transporting, and Preparing Food Safely" (page 18) for more information on proper storage and safe storage times for perishable foods.

Keep things simple by planning to use some of the same ingredients in more than one dish rather than packing your entire pantry. Many of the recipes in this book call for common pantry items such as garlic, onions, lemons, and so on.

Keep in mind that without the modern conveniences of a home kitchen, the end result is entirely dependent on the quality of your ingredients. Always choose the freshest meat and produce you can find, and steer clear of processed or prepared foods. (I make exceptions for canned beans, tomatoes, chicken broth, tuna, and the like, which are lifesavers on a long camping trip.)

Here are some sample meal plans, along with forms you can copy and use to plan your own meals and shopping lists.

SAMPLE MEAL PLAN FOR A THREE-DAY TRIP

Breakfast #1
Peanut Butter Pancakes (variation on
  Real Homemade Pancakes, page 67)
Coffee or tea
Orange juice

Lunch #1
Smoked Turkey Aram Sandwiches
  (page 89)
Raisins and nuts

Breakfast #2
Skillet Scones (page 70)
Coffee or tea
Orange juice

Lunch #2
Roast Beef and Horseradish Aram
  Sandwiches (page 88)
Carrot and celery sticks

Breakfast #3
Scrambled eggs
Hash brown potatoes (made from leftover
  Olive Oil Roasted Potatoes)
Coffee or tea
Orange juice

Lunch #3
Curried Chicken Salad Sandwiches (page
  79, using leftover Grilled Whole Chicken)
Fresh fruit

Snack #1
Baba Ghanoush (page 113)
Pita

Dinner #1
Orange-Herb Salmon (page 130)
Middle Eastern Salad (page 97)
Baked Bananas with Cinnamon
  (variation on Baked Chocolate
  Bananas, page 183)

Snack #2
Savory Cheese S'mores (page 108)

Dinner #2
Grilled Whole Chicken with Garlic Herb
  Butter (page 136)
Olive Oil Roasted Potatoes (page 177)
Grilled Asparagus (page 169)
Rum-Baked Peaches (page 186)

Snack #3
Tropical Fruit Salsa (page 104)
Chips

Dinner #3
Grilled Steak with Five-Spice Rub
  (page 148)
Black Bean Salad (page 92)
S'moradillas (page 187)

SAMPLE VEGETARIAN MEAL PLAN FOR A THREE-DAY TRIP

Breakfast #1
Peanut Butter Pancakes (variation on
Real Homemade Pancakes, page 67)
Coffee or tea
Orange juice

Lunch #1
Pesto and Vegetable Aram
Sandwiches (page 90)
Raisins and nuts

Snack #1
Parmesan Baked Apples (page 111)

Dinner #1
Grilled Portobello Burgers with Olive-
Herb Aioli (page 120)
Baked Bananas with Cinnamon
(variation on Baked Chocolate
Bananas, page 183)

Breakfast #2
Veggie Polenta Scramble (page 75)
Coffee or tea
Orange juice

Lunch #2
Peanut butter and banana sandwiches
Sliced bell peppers (red, orange,
yellow)

Snack #2
Savory Cheese S'mores (page 108)

Dinner #2
Tofu Steaks with Red Wine–
Mushroom Sauce (page 157)
Grilled Asparagus (page 169)
Maple-Caramel Baked Apples
(page 185)

Breakfast #3
Oatmeal
Coffee or tea
Orange juice

Lunch #3
California Grilled Cheese Sandwiches
(page 82)
Fresh fruit

Snack #3
Simply Perfect Guacamole (page 103)
Chips

Dinner #3
Goat Cheese Quesadillas (page 164)
with Tropical Fruit Salsa (page 104)
Black Bean Salad (page 92)
Baked Chocolate Bananas (page 183)

MEAL PLANNING FORM

Make copies of this form and fill out one for each day of your trip.

Day
_____

Breakfast
_____
_____

Who's cooking?
_____

Lunch
_____
_____

Who's cooking?
_____

Snack
_____
_____

Who's cooking?
_____

Dinner
_____
_____
_____

Who's cooking?
_____

SHOPPING LIST

Make copies of this form and use it to plan your shopping.

Supplies
_____
_____
_____

Dry Goods
_____
_____
_____

Canned and Jarred Food
_____
_____

Bread and Other Baked Goods
_____
_____

Dairy
_____
_____
_____

Meat
_____
_____

Frozen Foods
_____
_____
_____

Miscellaneous
_____
_____

PART II

THE RECIPES

Above all, camp cooking should be quick and easy. I've created the following recipes with that in mind—painstakingly paring down beloved classics and my own current favorite dishes to do away with superfluous ingredients and techniques. All of the recipes included here require mere minutes of preparation time and use only those ingredients necessary to bring out their unique characteristics. Since my goal is to deliver recipes that are not only easy enough for camping but delicious enough that you would be proud to serve them at home, I've included "Make It at Home" instructions in sidebars throughout the recipe section that offer tips for adapting the recipes to the home kitchen, as well as variations and enhancements that would be impractical for the camp kitchen but make the dishes even more special.

KEY TO SYMBOLS

vegetarian

no-cook

grill

camp stove

either grill or camp stove can be used

both grill and camp stove required

TABLE OF CONDIMENTS: SALAD DRESSINGS, SAUCES, MARINADES, AND MORE

Sometimes a condiment or sauce is a crucial element in a dish; other times it's just an added bonus. Either way, a well-seasoned sauce, dressing, or spread can turn an ordinary meal into something truly special. Following are recipes for sauces, salad dressings, marinades, spice rubs, dips, and spreads. Each was created to complement one or more specific dishes in this book, but most can be adapted and used in other ways to add variety to your camp cooking.

Dressings

BASIC VINAIGRETTE DRESSING

The type of vinegar you choose can completely transform this simple, classic vinaigrette. Try it with red or white wine vinegar, sherry vinegar, champagne vinegar, balsamic vinegar, or vinegar flavored with herbs or fruit. The possibilities are endless.

   1/4 cup vinegar of your choice
   I teaspoon Dijon mustard
   1/2 teaspoon sugar
   1/2 teaspoon salt
   1/2 teaspoon pepper
   1/2 cup olive oil

Mix the vinegar, mustard, sugar, salt, and pepper in a small bowl or jar. Whisk in the oil until the mixture is well blended.

Makes about 3/4 cup

MAKE IT AT HOME

Prepare any of these dressings as directed and store in the refrigerator. Bring to room temperature before serving. The dressings can be made several days ahead.

Variations:
- Add I large clove garlic, minced.
- Add I tablespoon chopped fresh herbs (basil, thyme, rosemary, tarragon, oregano, or a combination).
- Add I small shallot, minced.

HONEY-LEMON VINAIGRETTE

This light, flavorful dressing is good on anything from a simple salad of mixed greens to more elaborate blends of vegetables, fruit, and cheese.

Juice of 2 lemons
1/2 teaspoon salt
1/2 teaspoon pepper
1 tablespoon honey
1/3 cup olive oil, or more to taste

Mix all the ingredients in a small bowl or jar.

Makes about 2/3 cup

CITRUS SALAD DRESSING

Toss this simple tangy dressing with mixed greens and sliced tomatoes for a slighty exotic salad.

Juice and zest of 1 lime
Juice and zest of 1 lemon
1/2 teaspoon salt
1 teaspoon sugar
1 teaspoon ground cumin
1/4 cup olive oil

Mix the citrus juice and zest, salt, sugar, and cumin in a small bowl or jar until the salt and sugar dissolve. Whisk in the olive oil.

Makes about 3/4 cup

Marinades

Marinades are used to flavor and tenderize meat, poultry, fish, and vegetables before cooking. Generally, marinades contain three types of ingredients: acid (wine or spirits, vinegar, or citrus juice), which serves to tenderize the food as well as flavor it; aromatics, such as garlic or spices, which add strong flavor elements to the dish; and oils or fats, which hold the flavoring ingredients in contact with the food.

Marinating times vary widely for different foods, depending on how sturdy they are. Delicate foods such as fish and seafood require very little time, while tougher meats can be marinated for several days.

Most marinades can be made several days ahead and stored in a small jar or plastic container until you are ready to use them. If you plan to marinate the meat right away, mix the marinade ingredients in a large ziplock bag. Add the meat to the bag, seal it shut, shake to make sure the meat is well coated, and store in the cooler until you're ready to cook.

All the marinade recipes here make enough for up to 2 pounds of meat.

> **MAKE IT AT HOME**
>
> Each of these marinades can be made ahead and stored, covered, for up to a week in the refrigerator.

HONEY-SOY MARINADE 🫑

This simple sauce makes chicken wings irresistible, and it's also great on salmon, shrimp, and pork.

    3/4 cup soy sauce
    6 green onions, thinly sliced
    1/2 cup rice vinegar
    1/3 cup honey or brown sugar
    2 tablespoons peeled and chopped fresh ginger
    3 cloves garlic, minced
    2 tablespoons sesame oil

Mix all the ingredients until well combined.

GREEK MARINADE 🫑

This herb and lemon marinade is great on chicken, fish, or lamb.

   3 cloves garlic, minced
   Juice and zest of 2 lemons
   1/4 cup chopped fresh oregano
   2 tablespoons honey
   1/2 cup olive oil
   2 teaspoons salt
   1 1/2 teaspoons pepper

Mix all the ingredients until well combined.

MAPLE-GINGER MARINADE 🫑

This sweet marinade is ideal for pork but also goes well with duck, chicken, or salmon. Marinate salmon no longer than 30 minutes.

   1/2 cup soy sauce
   1/4 cup maple syrup
   1 tablespoon olive oil
   1 tablespoon peeled and minced fresh ginger
   1 tablespoon orange zest

Mix all the ingredients until well combined.

RED WINE MARINADE 🫑

This simple but flavorful marinade is perfect for steak.

   Juice of 3 limes or 2 lemons
   1/2 cup red wine
   2 cloves garlic, chopped
   1 tablespoon dried oregano
   1 teaspoon salt
   1 teaspoon pepper

Mix all the ingredients until well combined.

TEQUILA-LIME MARINADE 🌶️

Great for shrimp, this marinade works well with any seafood or fish, as well as chicken or pork. Marinate seafood or fish for 20 to 30 minutes.

    I cup tequila (rum or white wine are fine substitutes)
    Juice of 4 limes
    1/4 cup soy sauce
    1/4 cup packed brown sugar

Mix all the ingredients until well combined.

THAI MARINADE 🌶️*

This spicy marinade pairs well with any light meat. Try it on chicken, pork, fish, or tofu. Whatever you choose, plain rice and Thai Cabbage Salad (see recipe, page 99) will round out the meal nicely.

    I 14-ounce can unsweetened light coconut milk
    2 tablespoons Thai fish sauce (soy sauce may be substituted)
    Juice of I lime
    I tablespoon fresh ginger, minced
    2 serrano chiles, seeded and finely chopped
    I teaspoon salt

Mix all the ingredients until well combined.

* Recipe is vegetarian if prepared with soy sauce instead of fish sauce.

Spice Rubs

Spice rubs, also called "dry marinades," can be mixed ahead of time and stored indefinitely in ziplock bags or jars. When making spice rubs ahead, omit fresh ingredients such as garlic and fresh herbs, and add them just before using. I like to store spice rubs in ziplock bags with the name written right on the bag, along with any additions that need to be made before use.

Use these as you would a liquid marinade, to flavor meat, poultry, or fish. Simply combine the ingredients, rub the mixture all over the food to be flavored, seal, and chill until ready to cook.

All the spice rub recipes here make enough to flavor up to 2 pounds of meat, poultry, or fish.

BASIC BARBECUE SPICE RUB

This simple spice mixture, especially good for chicken, can be used for just about any meat or poultry.

    2 tablespoons brown sugar
    1 tablespoon paprika
    1 tablespoon dried sage
    1 1/2 teaspoons ground cumin
    1/2 to 1 teaspoon cayenne
    1 tablespoon salt
    1 teaspoon pepper

Mix all the ingredients until well combined.

CAJUN SPICE RUB 🌶

This spice rub is a great complement to pork, chicken, and even fish or shrimp. Make up a large batch—omitting the garlic—and you'll always be ready for a New Orleans–style feast. (Just remember to add the garlic before rubbing the mixture on your meat.)

    2 teaspoons paprika
    2 teaspoons dried oregano
    2 teaspoons pepper
    2 teaspoons ground cumin
    1/2 to 1 teaspoon cayenne
    2 teaspoons salt
    4 cloves garlic, minced

Mix all the ingredients until well combined.

MOROCCAN SPICE RUB 🌶

This intensely spicy rub, with hints of fennel and nutmeg, is best on steak or chicken. I like to rub it on flank steak, grill the steak medium rare, and serve it with Middle Eastern Salad (see recipe, page 97) and grilled sourdough bread with Olive Butter (see recipe, page 61).

    1 teaspoon pepper
    1 teaspoon crushed fennel seeds (crush seeds in a plastic bag,
       using an unopened can)
    1 teaspoon dry mustard
    1 teaspoon ground cumin
    1 teaspoon salt
    1/4 to 1/2 teaspoon cayenne
    1/4 teaspoon ground nutmeg
    2 cloves garlic, minced

Mix all the ingredients until well combined.

SOUTH-OF-THE-BORDER SPICE RUB 🫑

This spicy rub, quick and simple to prepare, adds serious zip to flank or skirt steak. Or try it with beef or chicken kebabs.

    2 tablespoons packed brown sugar
    1 tablespoon ground cumin
    1/2 tablespoon ground coriander
    1/2 tablespoon chili powder
    1/2 tablespoon salt
    1/2 tablespoon pepper
    1/2 teaspoon cinnamon
    1/4 to 1/2 teaspoon cayenne

Mix all the ingredients until well combined.

MIDDLE EASTERN SPICE RUB 🫑

Full of flavor, this minty rub is ideal for lamb. If you're making this ahead, leave out the garlic and mint (and be sure to add them before rubbing the mixture on your meat).

    1 tablespoon paprika
    1 tablespoon ground cumin
    1 tablespoon ground coriander
    1 teaspoon ground ginger
    1 teaspoon ground cinnamon
    1 tablespoon salt
    2 teaspoons pepper
    1/2 to 1 teaspoon cayenne
    3 cloves garlic, minced
    1/4 cup packed chopped fresh mint

Mix all the ingredients until well combined.

Balsamic Syrup

This sweet and tangy syrup is a perfect accompaniment for grilled vegetables (radicchio, cauliflower, squash) or for grilled chicken or fish.

1/4 cup packed brown sugar
1/2 cup water
1/2 cup balsamic vinegar
1 teaspoon salt

Cook the sugar, without stirring, in a small saucepan over medium heat on a camp stove, until melted (be careful not to let it burn). Carefully add the water, vinegar, and salt. Don't be concerned if the sugar hardens when you add the liquid. As the liquid heats up, the sugar will melt again and dissolve. Bring to a boil and continue to cook, stirring occasionally, 15 to 20 minutes, until the mixture is reduced to a syrupy consistency.

Makes about 3/4 cup

MAKE IT AT HOME

Prepare on the stove top as directed. You can make this several days ahead and store it, covered, in the refrigerator. Heat before serving.

Coconut Curry Sauce

This rich, flavorful sauce is delicious on grilled meat or tofu. I also like it drizzled over grilled cauliflower. This recipe makes enough for at least 2 pounds of meat, so if you're making less, either halve the recipe or plan to serve it on consecutive nights.

I 14-ounce can unsweetened light coconut milk
1/2 teaspoon salt
I tablespoon curry powder
I teaspoon ground coriander
1/4 to 1/2 teaspoon cayenne
1/4 cup peanut butter (preferably smooth)
2 tablespoons brown sugar
Juice of I lime

MAKE IT AT HOME

Prepare on the stove top as directed. You can make this up to a week ahead and store it, covered, in the refrigerator. Warm over medium heat before serving.

Mix all the ingredients in a small saucepan until well combined. Place over medium-high heat on a camp stove and bring the mixture to a boil. Lower the heat and simmer, stirring occasionally, about 10 minutes, until the sauce thickens.

Makes about 2 cups

Easy Red Wine Reduction Sauce

This classic sauce, traditionally served over pan-seared steak, couldn't be simpler to prepare. The key is using a good-quality wine. As the late, great Julia Child often said, you should never cook with a wine you wouldn't drink.

Use a light red wine, such as pinot noir, and try this sauce drizzled over chicken or even over heartier fishes such as salmon. This sauce is best if you incorporate the drippings from the meat or fish with which you plan to serve it. To do this, sear meat that has been seasoned with salt and pepper in a skillet, cooking to desired doneness. Set the meat aside. Remove all but about 1 tablespoon of the meat drippings from the pan and proceed with making the sauce.

> 2 tablespoons butter (plus 1 tablespoon if not using pan drippings)
> 1 medium shallot, finely chopped
> 1 tablespoon chopped fresh herbs (thyme or rosemary are good choices) or 1 teaspoon dried herbs (optional)
> 1/2 teaspoon salt
> 1/2 teaspoon pepper
> 2 1/4 cups red wine

If you're using pan drippings, cook the shallot over medium heat on a camp stove, in the skillet used to cook the meat, for about 3 minutes, until soft. If you're starting with a clean pan, melt 1 tablespoon of butter over medium heat, then add the shallot and cook about 3 minutes, until soft. Add the herbs, if using, along with the salt, pepper, and wine. Bring to a boil, lower the heat, and simmer 10 to 15 minutes, until reduced by about half. Just before serving, swirl 2 tablespoons of butter into the hot sauce.

Makes 1 1/2 cups

MAKE IT AT HOME

Prepare on the stove top as directed. If you're making this sauce ahead of time and want it to be even richer, start with a clean pan and add 1 cup rich veal or beef stock along with the wine. Simmer an additional 30 to 40 minutes, until the sauce is thick and syrupy.

* Recipe is vegetarian if prepared without meat or fish drippings.

Hoisin Glaze

This rich, tangy sauce works well with just about everything—tofu, chicken, fish, shrimp, scallops, beef, pork, and lamb.

1/2 cup hoisin sauce*
1/4 cup soy sauce
1/4 cup dry sherry, mirin,* or white wine
2 tablespoons sesame oil
2 tablespoons brown sugar or honey
1/2 teaspoon cayenne (optional)

Mix all the ingredients in a small bowl or jar until well combined.

If you desire, marinate meat in the mixture (time for marinating will depend on the meat you choose). While the meat is cooking, place the remaining marinade in a small saucepan and bring to a boil over medium-high heat. Cook, stirring frequently, at least 5 minutes or until sauce thickens. Serve drizzled over the grilled meat.

Makes about 1 1/4 cup

MAKE IT AT HOME

Prepare as directed. The glaze can be made up to 2 weeks ahead and kept, covered, in the refrigerator until ready to use.

* Hoisin sauce is a Chinese condiment and cooking ingredient made of ground soybeans, garlic, chiles, and spices. Mirin is a Japanese rice wine used for cooking. Find both in Asian markets or the Asian food aisles of many supermarkets.

Honey Mustard Sauce

This simple sauce works beautifully with salmon or as a dipping sauce for grilled chicken skewers.

> 1/4 cup Dijon mustard
> 1/3 cup olive oil
> 1/3 cup honey
> Juice of 1/2 lemon
> 1 1/2 teaspoons salt

Mix all the ingredients in a small bowl or jar until well combined.

Makes about 1 cup

Variations:

- Add 2 tablespoons of chopped fresh herbs such as rosemary, basil, or tarragon.
- Add 2 seeded and chopped jalapeños.

MAKE IT AT HOME

Prepare as directed. You can make the sauce up to 2 weeks ahead and keep it, covered, in the refrigerator until ready to use.

Spicy Peanut Sauce

Use this quick-to-prepare spicy sauce as a dip for grilled chicken, beef, vegetable, or shrimp kebabs, or toss it with hot noodles.

$1/2$ cup peanut butter (preferably smooth)

$1/4$ cup soy sauce

2 tablespoons sugar

2 tablespoons sesame oil

3 tablespoons rice vinegar

$1/4$ to $3/4$ teaspoon cayenne

$1/4$ cup water

MAKE IT AT HOME

Prepare as directed. You can make this sauce up to 1 week ahead and keep it, covered, in the refrigerator.

Mix all the ingredients in a small bowl until well combined.

Makes about $1^1/4$ cups

Variation:

For a fresh touch, add $1/2$ cup chopped fresh cilantro and/or 4 thinly sliced green onions.

Yogurt Mint Sauce

This flavorful sauce can be used to top grilled steak, lamb, chicken, or fish. Served with toasted pita triangles, it makes a nice appetizer.

1 cup plain yogurt
1/3 cup chopped fresh mint
1 large clove garlic, minced
1 tablespoon olive oil
1 teaspoon salt
1 large cucumber, peeled, seeded, and diced

Mix the yogurt, mint, garlic, olive oil, and salt in a medium bowl or saucepan. Stir the diced cucumber into the yogurt mixture. Serve immediately.

Makes about 2 1/2 cups

MAKE IT AT HOME

Instead of slicing the peeled and seeded cucumber, shred it in a food processor. Place the shredded cucumber in a colander and toss with 1 1/2 teaspoons of salt. Set aside for 20 to 30 minutes to draw out excess water. Turn the shredded cucumber out onto a dish towel or several layers of paper towels. Squeeze out as much moisture as possible. Proceed with preparation as above. You can make this sauce up to 2 days ahead and store it, covered, in the refrigerator until ready to use.

Easy Tomato Sauce

For comfort food on a cold night, there's nothing quite like a plate of steaming spaghetti with tomato sauce. Toss this sauce with cooked noodles and shave a bit of Parmesan cheese over the top. It is also a nice topping for Creamy Polenta (see recipe, page 181).

2 tablespoons olive oil
1 medium onion, diced
2 cloves garlic, minced
2 teaspoons dried oregano
1/2 teaspoon salt
1/2 teaspoon pepper
1/2 teaspoon sugar
1/2 teaspoon crushed red pepper (optional)
1 14-ounce can diced tomatoes, with juice
1 cup tomato purée
1/4 cup red wine (optional)

Heat the olive oil over medium heat in a medium pot on a camp stove. Add the onion and garlic, and cook, stirring, about 4 minutes, until the onion is soft and translucent. Add the oregano, salt, pepper, sugar, and crushed red pepper (if using). Cook about 30 seconds, then add the tomatoes and their juice, the tomato purée, and the wine (if using). Simmer 20 to 30 minutes, until the sauce is reduced by about one-third. Serve hot.

Makes about 3 cups

MAKE IT AT HOME

Use 8 medium fresh tomatoes, peeled and diced, in place of the canned tomatoes. Add 1/2 cup water or stock if needed. Omit the dried oregano. Add 2 to 3 tablespoons chopped fresh oregano after the sauce has reduced; then purée the sauce until smooth, if desired. You can make this sauce several days to a week ahead and store it, covered, in the refrigerator until ready to use.

Olive Relish

Tangy, sweet, salty, and spicy, this condiment can be used as a spread for crackers or crostini, paired with goat cheese or cream cheese for a tasty canapé, or used as a topping for grilled steak. Its strong flavors also pair well with sturdy fish such as swordfish, halibut, or mahimahi. Top fish fillets with a couple of tablespoons of the relish, and cook wrapped in foil over a hot fire.

 $1^1/_2$ cups pitted chopped kalamata olives
 3 tablespoons drained bottled capers, finely chopped
 1 tablespoon olive oil
 1 large garlic clove, minced
 Juice and zest of 1 orange
 1 tablespoon chopped fresh thyme or
  1 teaspoon crumbled dried thyme
 $^1/_4$ to $^1/_2$ teaspoon crushed red pepper
  flakes (optional)

Mix all the ingredients in a medium bowl until well combined.

Makes about $1^1/_2$ cups

MAKE IT AT HOME

Place all the ingredients in a food processor. Pulse to make a coarse purée. You can make this relish up to 2 weeks ahead and store it, covered, in the refrigerator until ready to serve. Bring to room temperature before serving.

Compound Butters

Compound butters—butters that have been softened and combined with other ingredients such as herbs and spices—are incredibly versatile condiments. Spread them on grilled bread, drop a pat onto a hot piece of grilled fish or meat for instant flavor, or use them to finish sauces.

These butters can be made ahead of time and stored in a well-chilled cooler or refrigerator for up to 2 weeks or in the freezer for several months. If not using immediately, turn the butter out onto a sheet of plastic wrap and form it into a log about 1½ inches in diameter. Wrap the log in plastic wrap, and chill until ready to use. Store in the freezer, in ziplock bags clearly marked with the type of butter and the date it was made.

ORANGE-HONEY BUTTER

This sweet butter is delicious on Skillet Scones (see recipe, page 70).

    1 stick (½ cup) butter, softened
    ¼ teaspoon salt (omit if using salted butter)
    Zest of 1 orange
    2 tablespoons honey

Mix all the ingredients in a small bowl until well combined.

GARLIC-HERB BUTTER

Use to top baked potatoes or grilled fish, chicken, steak, or mushrooms.

    1 stick (½ cup) butter, softened
    1½ teaspoons salt
    1 teaspoon pepper
    1 teaspoon crushed red pepper flakes
    4 cloves garlic, minced
    1 tablespoon chopped fresh rosemary
    1 tablespoon red wine (optional)

Mix all the ingredients in a small bowl until well combined.

GORGONZOLA BUTTER 🫑 🌿

The perfect topping for a plain grilled steak, this pungent butter is also delicious on baked potatoes, as a spread for grilled bread, or tossed with hot pasta.

    1 stick (1/2 cup) butter, softened
    1/2 cup crumbled Gorgonzola cheese (about 4 ounces)
    1 medium shallot, finely chopped
    2 tablespoons olive oil

Mix all the ingredients in a small bowl until well combined.

SPICY CHILI BUTTER 🫑 🔥

Delicious as a topping for baked yams, sweet potatoes, or corn on the cob, this butter also pairs well with grilled chicken or steak.

    1 stick (1/2 cup) butter, softened
    1 tablespoon chili powder
    1 tablespoon ground cinnamon
    1 1/2 teaspoons salt
    1/4 to 1 teaspoon cayenne

Mix all the ingredients in a small bowl until well combined.

OLIVE BUTTER 🫑 🌿

This butter is perfect on grilled steak, chicken, or fish, or spread on grilled bread.

    1 stick (1/2 cup) butter, softened
    1/4 cup pitted, chopped kalamata or other cured olives (about 10 large)
    1 tablespoon capers, finely chopped
    1/2 tablespoon chopped fresh thyme or 1/2 teaspoon crumbled
      dried thyme

Mix all the ingredients in a small bowl until well combined.

CHILE-LIME BUTTER

Use this tangy, spicy butter to top grilled fish, chicken, or beef. It also makes an ideal spread for corn on the cob.

    1 stick (1/2 cup) butter, softened
    2 serrano chiles, seeded and minced
    3 green onions, thinly sliced
    Juice and zest of 1 lime

Mix all the ingredients in a small bowl until well combined.

CHIPOTLE-HONEY BUTTER

Spicy, sweet, and smoky, this butter is a perfect complement to sweet grilled corn or sweet potatoes. It also makes a flavorful topping for salmon, chicken, or steak.

    1 stick (1/2 cup) butter, softened
    1/2 cup honey
    1/2 cup chopped cilantro
    2 tablespoons seeded and minced canned chipotle chiles in
      adobo*
    Juice of 1 lime
    1 teaspoon salt

Mix all the ingredients in a small bowl until well combined.

* Chipotle chiles are smoked jalapeños, usually sold canned in adobo sauce. Find them in Latin American food stores or the ethnic food aisle of many supermarkets.

Aioli

Traditionally, aioli is a garlicky, freshly made mayonnaise. The recipes below use various ingredients, from garlic and fresh herbs to spices and olives, to flavor store-bought mayonnaise. Use them as dips for seafood or vegetables, or as sandwich spreads. Be sure to keep all mayonnaise products cold.

Each of these recipes makes 3/4 to 1 cup.

NEOCLASSIC GARLIC AIOLI

Nothing livens up a tomato-based seafood stew like a dollop of garlic-spiked aioli. Try it with San Francisco Cioppino (see recipe, page 121), as a dipping sauce for grilled prawns, or as a spread for burgers and sandwiches.

> 3 garlic cloves, minced
> 3/4 cup mayonnaise
> 1/2 teaspoon salt

Mix all the ingredients in a small bowl until well combined. Cover and chill until ready to use.

LEMON AIOLI

Use this citrus mayonnaise to top grilled fish or veggies.

> 3/4 cup mayonnaise
> Juice and zest of 1 lemon
> 1/2 teaspoon salt

Mix all the ingredients in a small bowl until well combined. Cover and chill until ready to serve.

MAKE IT AT HOME

Easy enough to make at a campsite, aioli is even easier to make at home—just place all the ingredients in a food processor and process until well combined. Aioli can be made ahead and stored, tightly sealed, in the refrigerator for several days.

CHIPOTLE AIOLI 🫑 🔥

This spicy mayonnaise adds a nice kick to a burger or a grilled chicken sandwich, or you can serve it as a dipping sauce for barbecued prawns.

> 3/4 cup mayonnaise
> 1 minced chipotle chile from a can of chipotles in adobo,*
>   plus 1 tablespoon of the sauce
> 1/2 teaspoon salt

Mix all the ingredients in a small bowl until well combined. Cover and chill until ready to serve.

* Chipotle chiles are smoked jalapeños, usually sold canned in adobo sauce. Find them in Latin American food stores or the ethnic food aisle of many supermarkets.

FRESH HERB AIOLI 🫑 🔥

This fresh-flavored version is a perfect dipping sauce for fish or shellfish.

> 3/4 cup mayonnaise
> 1/3 cup finely chopped fresh herbs (basil, rosemary, chives,
>   or oregano)
> 2 cloves garlic, minced
> Juice and zest of 1 lemon
> 1/2 teaspoon salt

Mix all the ingredients in a small bowl until well combined. Cover and chill until ready to serve.

CHILE AND LIME AIOLI

This version is a zesty complement for grilled chicken sandwiches, turkey burgers, or grilled fish.

3/4 cup mayonnaise
1/3 cup finely chopped fresh cilantro
Juice and zest of 1 lime
1 serrano chile, seeded and minced
1/2 teaspoon salt

Mix all the ingredients in a small bowl until well combined. Cover and chill until ready to serve.

OLIVE AIOLI

Serve this salty version with grilled whitefish.

1/4 cup mayonnaise
1 garlic clove, minced
1/3 cup pitted and finely chopped cured black olives (about 12 large)
1 tablespoon minced fresh thyme or 1 teaspoon crumbled dried thyme

Mix all the ingredients in a small bowl until well combined. Cover and chill until ready to serve.

CHAPTER 7

START THE DAY RIGHT: BREAKFAST

Like it or not, when you're sleeping outdoors, you'll most likely wake with the sun. Dragging yourself from your cozy sleeping bag into the crisp morning air can feel like a painful chore, but the promise of a hot, delicious breakfast will make it much more appealing. For me, a hot cup of coffee is the ultimate motivator, and I've found that the most efficient brewing system in the wilderness is a French press. All you need to do is heat a pot of water on the camp stove, add it to coffee grounds in the pitcher, wait a few minutes, and voilà! You've got a nice strong cup of hot coffee. Once you've gotten your caffeine fix, making breakfast will be a breeze. Following are several recipes that will give you the energy you'll need for the active day ahead.

Real Homemade Pancakes

Why use store-bought mix when it's so easy to wow your friends and family with pancakes made from scratch? Keep these airy pancakes small for easy flipping.

 2 cups (one recipe) Multipurpose Baking Mix (see recipe, page 35)
 1/4 cup sugar
 2 cups milk (or as needed to achieve desired consistency)
 2 eggs, lightly beaten, or 1/2 cup egg substitute*
 Butter for cooking and serving
 Maple syrup for serving

Mix the baking mix, sugar, milk, and eggs in a large bowl until well combined.

Heat a large, heavy skillet over medium heat on a camp stove. Melt the butter, swirling to coat the pan. Ladle about 1/4 cup of the batter at a time into the pan. Cook each pancake on one side for about 4 minutes, until lots of large bubbles form on top and begin to burst. Flip each pancake, and continue cooking about 4 minutes more, until the bottom is browned. Serve hot with butter and maple syrup.

Serves 4

Variations:

- **Blueberry Pancakes** Prepare as above, sprinkling 1 tablespoon or so of fresh or frozen (unthawed is fine) blueberries onto each pancake just after ladling the batter onto the skillet.
- **Banana Pancakes** Prepare as above, stirring two chopped bananas into the batter before cooking.
- **Gingerbread Pancakes** Prepare as above, adding 2 teaspoons ground ginger and 1 teaspoon ground cinnamon to the batter before cooking.
- **Peanut Butter Pancakes** Prepare as above, adding an extra 1/4 cup milk and 3/4 cup smooth peanut butter to the batter.

* For long trips, I recommend egg substitute because the cartons are easy to store and will last a long time in a well-chilled cooler.

Bananas Foster French Toast

Who says you can't have dessert first thing in the morning? Sure it's indulgent—but you're on vacation, right?

- 1/4 cup (1/2 stick) butter, divided
- 1/4 cup packed brown sugar
- 3 medium bananas, peeled and diced
- 2 tablespoons dark rum
- 4 eggs
- 1 cup whole milk
- 1 teaspoon vanilla extract (optional)
- 8 thick slices bread

Melt 2 tablespoons of the butter in a saucepan over medium heat on a camp stove. Add the brown sugar and cook, stirring, until the sugar dissolves. Add the diced bananas and cook 1 or 2 minutes, until the pieces are heated through and begin to break down. Add the rum, bring to a boil (you may need to raise the heat), and cook, stirring, 1 minute more. Set aside.

Whisk together the eggs, milk, and vanilla (if using) in a medium bowl or pot. Submerge the bread slices (a couple at a time) in the egg mixture and let soak 1 or 2 minutes.

MAKE IT AT HOME

Topped with a crunchy banana-pecan crust and baked like a bread pudding, this makes an impressive dish for breakfast or brunch.

Banana-Pecan French Toast

Mix the eggs, milk, and vanilla. Place the bread slices in a single layer on a greased baking sheet, and pour the egg mixture over the top. Cover and chill at least 8 hours. Before cooking, preheat the oven to 400°F. Mix together 1/2 cup packed brown sugar; 1/2 cup pecans; 3 medium bananas, peeled and diced; and 2 tablespoons dark rum. Spread the pecan mixture over the top of the bread slices, and dot with butter. Bake, uncovered, about 20 minutes, until the pecan mixture is golden brown.

Heat 1 tablespoon of the butter in a large skillet over medium heat. Add 2 or 3 slices of the soaked bread at a time to the skillet, and cook about 3 minutes, until golden brown on the bottom. Turn over and cook another 3 minutes or so, until the bottoms are golden brown. Repeat with the remaining bread and egg mixture, adding more butter to the pan as needed. Serve hot, topped with some of the banana mixture.

Serves 4

Cook the bananas in a skillet, then set aside. Whisk together the eggs, milk, and vanilla, then submerge the bread slices in the mixture. Pan-fry the bread. Top with the cooked bananas.

Skillet Scones

Though the Brits might object to calling these little biscuits "scones" ("Scones are never made with eggs!" one scoffed at me recently), I've found the only way to keep them from tasting like burned-on-the-outside, doughy-in-the-middle hockey pucks is to add a lightly beaten egg to the batter. I suppose I should call them "skillet biscuits." But that just doesn't sound as good, does it?

These airy biscuits are a perfect foil for Orange-Honey Butter (see recipe, page 60). They're also great with butter and jam or just a drizzle of maple syrup. The trick in this recipe is cooking the scones at low enough heat that they cook through the middle before they burn on the outside.

> 2 cups (one recipe) Multipurpose Baking Mix (see recipe, page 35)
> 3 tablespoons sugar
> 3/4 cup buttermilk
> 1/2 cup (1 stick) melted butter, cooled
> 1 egg, lightly beaten, or 1/4 cup
>   egg substitute

Mix all the ingredients in a medium bowl or pot, using your hands, until a soft, sticky dough forms. Break off a chunk about the size of a golf ball, roll it into a ball between your palms, and then flatten it to about a 1/2-inch-thick, 2 1/2-inch-wide patty. Repeat with the remaining dough.

Spray a skillet with nonstick cooking spray or grease it with butter. Heat the skillet over medium-low heat. When the pan is hot, add the dough patties, pressing them down a bit as you put them in the pan, to make sure as much of the dough as possible is in contact with the pan. Cook, covered, turning the scones over after about 4 minutes, or when the bottoms have browned. Replace the lid and continue to cook about 4 minutes more, until the bottoms are golden brown and the biscuits are cooked through. (You may need to split one open to test for doneness.) Serve hot.

Makes about 16 small scones

Variations:

- **Dried Fruit Scones** Add 1/2 cup raisins, dried cranberries, currants, or other dried fruit to the batter before cooking.
- **Citrus Scones** Add 1 tablespoon lemon or orange zest to the batter before cooking.
- **Maple Scones** Substitute brown sugar for the sugar. Stir 1/3 cup maple syrup into the buttermilk before adding it to the flour mixture. Continue with preparation as directed.

MAKE IT AT HOME

Preheat the oven to 375°F. Prepare the dough as directed. Form the dough into 1 large patty, about 1 inch thick. Cut into 8 wedges, and place on a baking sheet. Bake the scones about 20 minutes, until golden brown. Serve warm.

Pan-Fried Bread with Pears, Blue Cheese, and Maple Syrup

I got the idea for this dish from a café in my neighborhood that serves a variation made with tart green apples. I prefer the subtle flavor and soft texture of pears, but any type of apple would be a fine substitution. I could eat this dish any time of day.

> 1/2 tablespoon butter, more if needed
>
> 2 slices whole wheat bread
>
> 2 ounces Gorgonzola, Cambazola, or other soft blue cheese
>
> 1/2 medium ripe pear, cored and thinly sliced
>
> 2 tablespoons maple syrup

Melt the butter in a skillet over medium heat on a camp stove. Place the bread in a single layer in the skillet, and cook until the underside is browned, about 3 minutes. Turn the bread over (add a little more butter, if needed), top with the cheese, and continue to cook until the underside is browned, about 3 minutes more. Remove from the pan, top with the pear slices, and drizzle with maple syrup. Serve immediately.

Serves 1

MAKE IT AT HOME

This dish can be prepared as directed, using the stove top, or the bread can be toasted in a toaster, as it is at the café. I like the richness and crunch that frying the bread in a touch of butter gives the dish, but dry toasting is a fine option.

Sausage and Polenta Scramble

Similar to Italian frittata or Spanish tortilla, this is an easy way to serve eggs to a crowd. The addition of ready-made polenta, which is sold in 18-ounce tubes at many supermarkets, makes this dish hearty and satisfying without making it heavy. Create variations by using different types of sausage or cheese and different herbs and spices.

6 eggs or 1½ cups liquid egg substitute
¼ cup milk
4 ounces shredded Monterey Jack cheese (about ½ cup)
½ teaspoon salt
¼ teaspoon pepper
½ teaspoon crushed red pepper (optional)
1 tablespoon olive oil
½ medium onion, diced
2 links smoked chicken sausage, halved lengthwise and sliced
4 ounces ready-made polenta, cut into ½-inch dice (about 1 cup)

Beat the eggs in a medium bowl or pot. Add the milk, cheese, salt, pepper, and red pepper (if using) and mix well. Set aside.

Heat the oil in a skillet over high heat on a camp stove. Add the onion and cook, stirring, about 2 minutes, until it is beginning to soften. Reduce the heat to medium-high, add

MAKE IT AT HOME

Preheat the broiler. Prepare the egg mixture as directed. Set aside.

Heat the oil in a large oven-safe skillet over high heat on the stove top. Add the onion and cook, stirring, about 2 minutes, until it is beginning to soften. Reduce the heat to medium-high, add the sausage, and continue cooking about 5 minutes more, until the onion is translucent. Add the polenta and cook, stirring, about 2 minutes more, until heated through. Spread the polenta mixture evenly in the pan, reduce the heat to medium-low, and pour the egg mixture evenly over the top. Cook, without stirring, for 8 to 10 minutes, or until the edge is set but the center is still soft.

Place the pan under the broiler. Cook 2 to 3 minutes, until the top is golden. Remove from the broiler and let the scramble cool in the skillet for a few minutes. Cut into wedges and serve warm or at room temperature.

the sausage, and continue cooking about 5 minutes more, until the onion is translucent. Add the polenta and cook, stirring, about 2 minutes more, until heated through. Spread the polenta mixture evenly in the pan, reduce the heat to medium-low, and pour the egg mixture evenly over the top. Cover and cook about 12 to 15 minutes, stirring once or twice during cooking, until cooked through. Serve immediately.

Serves 4

Veggie Polenta Scramble

This vegetarian frittata makes a hearty breakfast. Serve it cut into wedges with a spoonful of salsa, if desired.

6 eggs or 1 1/2 cups liquid egg substitute
1/4 cup milk
4 ounces shredded Monterey Jack cheese (about 1/2 cup)
1/2 teaspoon salt
1/4 teaspoon pepper
1 tablespoon chopped fresh rosemary or 1 teaspoon crumbled dried rosemary
1 tablespoon olive oil
1 medium onion, diced
2 cups chopped button mushrooms
1 large red bell pepper, seeded and diced
4 ounces ready-made polenta, cut into 1/2-inch dice (about 1 cup)

MAKE IT AT HOME

Preheat the broiler. Prepare as directed, cooking on the stove top without stirring until almost cooked through, 8 to 10 minutes. To finish, place the pan under the broiler and cook 2 to 3 minutes, until the top is golden. Remove from the broiler and let the scramble cool in the skillet for a few minutes. Cut into wedges and serve warm or at room temperature.

Beat the eggs in a medium bowl or pot. Add the milk, cheese, salt, pepper, and rosemary and mix well. Set aside.

Heat the oil in a skillet over high heat on a camp stove. Add the onion and cook, stirring, about 2 minutes, until it is beginning to soften. Reduce the heat to medium-high, add the mushrooms and bell pepper, and cook about 5 minutes more, until the onion is translucent and the mushrooms and pepper soften. Add the polenta and cook, stirring, about 2 minutes more, until heated through. Spread the polenta mixture evenly in the pan, reduce the heat to medium-low, and pour the egg mixture over the top. Cover and cook about 12 to 15 minutes, stirring it up once or twice during cooking, until cooked through. Serve immediately.

Serves 4

Mediterranean Breakfast Wrap

Packed with the flavors of the sunny Mediterranean, these wraps will get your day started right. For extra nutrition and crunch, add a handful of baby spinach leaves to each wrap before rolling.

6 eggs or 1½ cups liquid egg substitute
1 teaspoon crumbled dried oregano
½ teaspoon salt
½ teaspoon pepper
1 tablespoon milk (optional)
1 to 2 tablespoons olive oil or butter
4 tortillas
4 ounces goat cheese (about ½ cup)
¼ cup pitted, chopped olives
¼ cup drained, chopped sun-dried tomatoes (oil-packed)

MAKE IT AT HOME

Prepare on the stove top as directed.

Beat the eggs in a medium bowl with the oregano, salt, pepper, and milk (if using). Heat the oil or butter in a skillet over medium heat on a camp stove. Add the eggs to the skillet and reduce the heat to low. Cook the eggs, stirring often, 3 to 5 minutes, until cooked to the desired doneness.

While the eggs are cooking, spread one-quarter (about 1 ounce) of the goat cheese down the center of each tortilla. Top with the olives and sun-dried tomatoes.

Spoon the cooked eggs onto the tortillas on top of the cheese, olives, and tomato, dividing evenly among the 4 tortillas. Roll the tortillas into neat packages by folding the ends in first, then rolling into a cylinder.

Wipe out the skillet with a paper towel. Add a little more butter or oil, and warm over medium heat. When the pan is hot, add the rolled-up tortillas, seam-side down. Cook about 2 minutes, until the undersides are golden brown. Turn the wraps over and cook another 2 minutes or so, until the undersides are golden brown. Serve immediately.

Serves 4

Lox and Cream Cheese Breakfast to Go

I bet even your *bubbe* would approve of this twist on the traditional lox-and-bagel breakfast. If you want to get up and out for an early hike, make these compact wraps the night before and store, tightly wrapped in plastic wrap, in your cooler. In the morning, just grab them and go. Make them using either lavash,* a Middle Eastern flatbread, or flour tortillas.

1 1/2 24-9-inch sheets lavash or 4 10-inch flour tortillas
1 1/2 cups cream cheese
8 ounces thinly sliced smoked salmon
2 medium tomatoes, thinly sliced
1/2 red onion, thinly sliced
1/4 cup capers

Spread the cream cheese evenly over the lavash. Place a layer of smoked salmon over the cream cheese, then a layer of tomato slices, then onion, then capers. Tightly roll the flatbread or tortillas around the filling into a cylinder, and slice into 4- or 5-inch pieces. Serve immediately, or wrap tightly in plastic wrap or aluminum foil.

MAKE IT AT HOME
Prepare as directed. Slice into 2-inch pieces and serve as an appetizer.

Serves 4

Variation:
Substitute herbed cream cheese for the plain cream cheese mixture.

* Lavash is available in specialty food stores and the ethnic food aisle of many supermarkets.

CHAPTER 8
MIDDAY MEALS: SANDWICHES, SALADS, AND SUCH

If you're anything like me, you'll be starving by midday from all the hiking and exploring you'll be doing. For a day-long hike, make lunch ahead and bring it along—try some of the wraps in this chapter, or on cold days try cooking up a few of the grilled sandwiches while you prepare breakfast, and wrap them in foil to keep them warm on your morning adventures. If you're spending your day lounging around the campsite, try some of the salads or more complicated sandwiches for a midday meal.

Curried Chicken Salad Sandwiches

This is a great way to use up any leftover grilled chicken from the previous night's dinner. You can substitute two 6-ounce cans of solid white tuna (drained) for the chicken.

3/4 pound diced or shredded cooked chicken (about 1 1/2 cups)
1/3 cup mayonnaise
1 teaspoon Dijon mustard
1/2 teaspoon salt
2 tablespoons curry powder
1/3 cup raisins
1/3 cup slivered almonds or roasted, unsalted pistachios
8 slices whole wheat bread or 4 8-inch round pitas
4 large lettuce leaves, torn in half or shredded

Mix the chicken, mayonnaise, mustard, salt, curry powder, raisins, and nuts in a medium bowl until well combined. Make 4 sandwiches, dividing the chicken mixture evenly among them and topping each with lettuce. Serve immediately, or wrap prepared sandwiches tightly in plastic wrap or aluminum foil and store in a cooler or insulated lunch bag.

Serves 4

MAKE IT AT HOME

Prepare the chicken salad as directed. Cover and store in the refrigerator until ready to serve (can be made up to 2 days ahead). Assemble the sandwiches just before serving.

Tuna and Olive Salad Sandwiches

Olives and roasted peppers add tons of flavor to a basic tuna salad. If your olives have pits, just smash the olives with the side of a large knife blade or an unopened jar or can. They'll break open so you can pop the pits right out.

2 6-ounce cans solid white tuna, drained

1/4 cup mayonnaise

Juice of 1/2 lemon

1 teaspoon Dijon mustard

1/2 cup drained and chopped roasted red peppers from a jar (about 1 bell pepper)

1/3 cup coarsely pitted, chopped kalamata or other brine-cured olives

2 ribs celery, chopped

8 slices whole wheat bread or 4 8-inch pita rounds

1 medium tomato, thinly sliced

4 lettuce leaves

Mix the tuna, mayonnaise, lemon juice, mustard, peppers, olives, and celery in a medium bowl or pot until well combined. Make 4 sandwiches with the bread, tuna mixture, tomato slices, and lettuce.

Serves 4

MAKE IT AT HOME

Prepare the tuna salad as directed. Cover and chill until ready to serve (can be made up to 2 days ahead). Assemble the sandwiches just before serving.

Prosciutto, Goat Cheese, and Fig Sandwiches

These sophisticated sandwiches are perfect for taking along on a hike or for putting together to eat at the campsite.

8 slices hearty Italian or sourdough bread
8 ounces goat cheese
4 ripe but firm black mission figs, stemmed and sliced
4 thin slices Italian prosciutto or ham
1/4 cup chopped fresh mint leaves (optional)

Toast the bread over a hot fire, if desired, 2 to 3 minutes per side, until golden brown. Lay 4 slices of bread on your work surface, and spread each with one-quarter (about 2 ounces) of the cheese. Top each slice with one-quarter of the fig slices and 1 slice of prosciutto. Sprinkle with chopped mint, if using, and top with the remaining slices of bread. Serve immediately or wrap tightly in plastic wrap.

Serves 4

California Grilled Cheese Sandwiches

Everyone loves a toasty, cheesy, grilled cheese sandwich. Make them in the morning, wrap them up in foil just after grilling, and they'll stay warm until lunchtime. These sandwiches can be cooked either on the grill or in a skillet on a camp stove.

2/3 cup finely chopped drained canned artichoke hearts
1/3 cup finely chopped drained oil-packed sun-dried tomatoes
1/3 cup finely chopped pitted cured olives
1/2 teaspoon salt
1/2 teaspoon pepper
Olive oil spray or nonstick cooking spray (for grill method) or
    2 tablespoons butter or olive oil (for camp-stove method)
8 slices San Francisco sourdough bread
8 ounces Monterey Jack cheese, thinly sliced

Mix the artichoke hearts, sun-dried tomatoes, olives, salt, and pepper in a small bowl until well combined.

GRILL METHOD:

Spray one side of each slice of bread with olive oil. Place 4 slices on your work surface, oiled-side down, and spread one-quarter of the artichoke mixture on each. Top each with one-quarter (about 2 ounces) of the cheese. Place the remaining 4 slices of bread on top, oiled side up.

Put the sandwiches directly on the grill over high heat, and cook 3 to 4 minutes, until the undersides are golden brown and the cheese has begun to melt. Carefully turn over the sandwiches. Cook 3 to 4 minutes more, until the bottoms are golden brown. Turn the sandwiches again, and cook about 1 more minute, until the cheese has melted completely. Slice each sandwich in half and serve immediately or wrap tightly in foil.

CAMP-STOVE METHOD:

Do not spray the bread with oil. Lay 4 slices of the bread on your work surface. Top each with one-quarter of the artichoke mixture, then one-quarter (about 2 ounces) of the cheese. Place the remaining 4 slices of bread on top.

Heat the olive oil or melt the butter in a skillet over medium-high heat on the camp stove. Add sandwiches in a single layer (you'll have to cook them in batches), cover, and cook 2 to 3 minutes, until the undersides are golden brown and the cheese has begun to melt. Carefully turn over the sandwiches. Cook 2 to 3 minutes more, until the bottoms are golden brown. Turn over the sandwiches again, and cook 1 more minute or so until the cheese has melted completely. Slice each sandwich in half and serve immediately or wrap tightly in foil.

Serves 4

Mix the filling in a bowl, then top the bread with it and the cheese.
Cook in a skillet for about 2 to 3 minutes per side.

Grilled Goat Cheese Sandwich with Shallot, Tomato, and Thyme

This sandwich was inspired by my neighborhood crepe shack, which serves the light pancakes filled with a sublime ragout of shallots, tomatoes, and fresh thyme with a dollop of tangy goat cheese.

Olive oil spray or nonstick cooking spray (for grill method)
'or 2 tablespoons olive oil or butter (for camp stove method)
8 slices French, Italian, or sourdough bread
8 ounces goat cheese (about 1 cup)
1 medium shallot, very thinly sliced
1 1/2 tablespoons chopped fresh thyme
1 large tomato, thinly sliced
1/2 teaspoon salt
1/2 teaspoon pepper

GRILL METHOD:

Spray one side of each slice of bread with olive oil. Place 4 slices on your work surface, oiled side down, and spread one-quarter (about 2 ounces) of the cheese on each. Distribute the shallot and thyme evenly among the 4 slices. Top each slice with 2 slices of tomato, and sprinkle with salt and pepper. Place the remaining 4 slices of bread on top, oiled side up.

Put the sandwiches directly on the grill over high heat. Cook 3 to 4 minutes, until the undersides are golden brown and the cheese has begun to melt. Carefully turn over the sandwiches. Cook 3 to 4 minutes more, until the bottoms are golden brown. Turn the sandwiches again, and cook about 1 more minute, until the cheese has melted completely. Serve immediately or wrap tightly in foil.

CAMP-STOVE METHOD:

Do not spray the bread with oil. Lay 4 slices of the bread on your work surface. Top each with one-quarter (about 2 ounces) of the cheese. Distribute the shallot and thyme evenly among the 4 slices. Top each slice with 2 slices of tomato, and sprinkle with salt and pepper. Place the remaining 4 slices of bread on top.

Heat the olive oil or melt the butter in a skillet over medium-high heat on the camp stove. Add sandwiches in a single layer (you'll have to cook them in batches), cover, and cook 2 to 3 minutes, until the undersides are golden brown and the cheese has begun to melt. Carefully turn over the sandwiches. Cook 2 to 3 minutes more, until the bottoms are golden brown. Turn over the sandwiches again, and cook about 1 more minute, until the cheese has melted completely. Slice each sandwich in half. Serve immediately or wrap tightly in foil.

MAKE IT AT HOME

Prepare and cook the sandwiches according to the camp-stove method, using the stove top.

Serves 4

Hot and Spicy California Grilled Cheese

These spicy sandwiches combine California's best ingredients—creamy avocados, tart lime juice, and the spicy south-of-the-border influence of smoky chipotle chiles.

> 1 large avocado
> 1/2 teaspoon salt
> 1 minced chipotle chile from a can of chipotles in adobo sauce*
> 2 green onions, thinly sliced
> Juice of 1/2 lime
> 8 slices multigrain bread
> Olive oil spray or nonstick cooking spray
> 8 ounces Monterey Jack or sharp cheddar cheese, thinly sliced

Mash the avocado in a small bowl with the salt, chile, green onion, and lime juice.

MAKE IT AT HOME

Prepare and cook the sandwiches according to the camp-stove method, using the stove top.

GRILL METHOD:

Spray one side of each slice of bread with olive oil. Place 4 slices on your work surface, oiled-side down, and spread each with one-quarter of the avocado mixture. Distribute the cheese evenly among the four slices. Place the remaining 4 slices of bread on top, oiled-side up.

Put the sandwiches directly on the grill over high heat, and cook 3 to 4 minutes, until the undersides are golden brown and the cheese has begun to melt. Carefully turn over the sandwiches. Cook about 3 minutes more, until the bottoms are golden brown. Turn the sandwiches again. Cook about 1 more minute, until the cheese has melted completely. Slice each sandwich in half. Serve immediately or wrap tightly in foil.

CAMP-STOVE METHOD:

Do not spray the bread with oil. Lay 4 slices of the bread on your work surface, and spread each with one-quarter of the avocado mixture. Distribute the cheese evenly among the 4 slices. Place the remaining 4 slices of bread on top.

Heat the olive oil or melt the butter in a skillet over medium-high heat on the camp stove. Add sandwiches in a single layer (you'll have to cook them in batches), cover, and cook 2 to 3 minutes, until the undersides are golden brown and the cheese has begun to melt. Carefully turn over the sandwiches. Cook 2 to 3 minutes more, until the bottoms are golden brown. Turn over the sandwiches again, and cook about 1 more minute, until the cheese has melted completely. Slice each sandwich in half. Serve immediately or wrap tightly in foil.

Serves 4

* Chipotle chiles are smoked jalapeños, usually sold canned in adobo sauce. Find them in Latin American food stores or the ethnic food aisle of many supermarkets.

Aram Sandwiches

These compact rolled sandwiches are traditionally made using lavash,* a Middle Eastern flat bread, but flour tortillas make a fine substitute and are much easier to find.

To prepare, spread the cheese over the tortillas, dividing evenly among them. Layer the other ingredients on top. Tightly roll each tortilla into a cylinder around the filling. Slice each cylinder in half to serve.

If you use lavash for these sandwiches, to make 4 servings, use 1 full 24- by 9-inch sheet and 1 sheet cut in half so that it is 12 inches by 9 inches. Prepare with the long side of the bread facing you. Then roll up so that you have a 24-inch cylinder and a 12-inch cylinder. Slice each into 4-inch lengths to serve.

Make up your own combinations or try the ones below.

MAKE IT AT HOME

All the Aram Sandwiches can be made at home as directed in the recipes. Cut them into 2-inch lengths and serve them as appetizers, if desired.

* Lavash is available in specialty food stores or the ethnic food aisle or bread aisle of many supermarkets.

ROAST BEEF AND HORSERADISH ARAM SANDWICHES

A classic combination of roast beef and horseradish in a "newfangled" package.

   1½ cups (12 ounces) cream cheese mixed with 1½ tablespoons
      prepared horseradish
   4 10-inch flour tortillas
   8 ounces thinly sliced roast beef
   1 red bell pepper, seeded and thinly sliced
   4 leaves romaine lettuce

Prepare according to the directions above.

Serves 4

SMOKED SALMON AND WASABI ARAM SANDWICHES

The punch of wasabi paste gives these wraps a Japanese flair, but horse-radish is a fine substitute.

    1$\frac{1}{2}$ cups (12 ounces) cream cheese mixed with 1 tablespoon
       prepared wasabi paste* or prepared horseradish
    4 10-inch flour tortillas
    8 ounces thinly sliced smoked salmon
    $\frac{1}{2}$ medium cucumber, peeled and thinly sliced
    2 tablespoons minced fresh chives or 3 green onions, thinly
       sliced

Prepare according to the directions above.

Variation:

Substitute herbed cream cheese for the wasabi–cream cheese mixture.

Serves 4

* Wasabi, a spicy Japanese horseradish, is available in the Asian food section of most supermarkets.

SMOKED TURKEY ARAM SANDWICHES

A flavorful variation of the tired turkey and cheese sandwich, this simple wrap makes a perfect take-along meal.

    1$\frac{1}{2}$ cups (12 ounces) herbed cream cheese
    4 10-inch flour tortillas
    8 ounces thinly sliced smoked turkey
    2 medium tomatoes, thinly sliced
    $\frac{1}{2}$ medium cucumber, peeled and thinly sliced

Prepare according to the directions above.

Serves 4

ROASTED VEGETABLE ARAM SANDWICHES

This wrap offers a great way to use up leftover grilled vegetables from the previous night's dinner. Any grilled vegetables can be substituted for those listed here.

>   3/4 cup (6 ounces) cream cheese mixed with 3/4 cup (about
>   6 ounces) goat cheese
>   4 10-inch flour tortillas
>   1/2 cup sliced roasted red bell pepper, from a jar
>   2 grilled thinly sliced zucchini
>   1 cup shredded romaine lettuce

Prepare according to the directions above.

Serves 4

PESTO AND VEGETABLE ARAM SANDWICHES

Store-bought pesto quickly livens up a simple veggie wrap.

>   1 1/2 cups (12 ounces) cream cheese mixed with 2 tablespoons
>   purchased pesto
>   4 10-inch flour tortillas
>   2 medium tomatoes, thinly sliced
>   4 leaves romaine lettuce

Prepare according to the directions above.

Serves 4

Grilled Peach and Arugula Salad with Goat Cheese

This salad is a great way to highlight summer peaches. Nectarines or apricots can be substituted, if desired. Be sure whatever fruit you choose is perfectly ripe.

    2 large peaches, pits removed, sliced $1/2$ inch thick
    4 cups arugula or baby spinach leaves
    Honey-Lemon Vinaigrette (see recipe, page 44)
    4 ounces goat cheese, crumbled (about $1/2$ cup)
    $1/2$ cup crushed pecans

Grill the peach slices over high heat, 2 to 3 minutes per side, until they have begun to brown and soften. Chop into $1/2$-inch chunks and toss, in a medium bowl or pot, with the arugula and vinaigrette. Sprinkle the goat cheese and pecans over the top and serve.

Serves 4

MAKE IT AT HOME

Grill the peach slices in a ridged grill pan over medium-high heat on the stove top. Garnish with Spiced Pecans for a special touch.

Spiced Pecans

Preheat the oven to 375°F. Blanch $1 1/2$ cups pecans in boiling water for 5 minutes, and drain well. Toss the nuts with $1/4$ cup sugar, 1 teaspoon salt, and $1/2$ teaspoon cayenne, and spread on a baking sheet. Toast in the oven, stirring occasionally, about 15 minutes, or until crunchy. Spread the nuts on waxed paper to cool. These can be made ahead and stored in an airtight container for several weeks.

Black Bean Salad

This salad benefits from marinating for several hours and only improves with time, so consider making it up to 2 days ahead and packing it, well-sealed, in your cooler. Serve it alongside Grilled Steak Tacos (see recipe, page 151) or Goat Cheese Quesadillas (see recipe, pages 164). Add 2 cups of diced, cooked chicken, shrimp, or smoked tofu to make the salad a meal in itself.

Juice of 3 limes
1 teaspoon salt
2 tablespoons honey
1 tablespoon ground cumin
1 tablespoon ground coriander
1 tablespoon dried oregano
2 14.5-ounce cans black beans, drained and rinsed
2 bell peppers (preferably red, yellow, or orange, or a
    combination), seeded and diced
6 green onions, thinly sliced

Mix the lime juice, salt, honey, cumin, coriander, and oregano in a large bowl until well combined. Add the beans, diced pepper, and onion, and toss until well combined. If you're making this ahead, cover and store in a cooler. Bring to room temperature before serving.

Serves 4

Creole Slaw

The addition of cayenne and horseradish makes this an interesting change from traditional coleslaw.

1 1/2 tablespoons Dijon mustard
2 teaspoons prepared horseradish
3 tablespoons wine vinegar (red or white)
1/4 cup mayonnaise
1 teaspoon salt
1 teaspoon sugar
1/4 to 1/2 teaspoon cayenne
1 large head green cabbage, shredded

Mix the mustard, horseradish, vinegar, mayonnaise, salt, sugar, and cayenne in a large bowl until well combined. Add the cabbage, toss until well combined, and serve.

Serves 4

MAKE IT AT HOME

Prepare as directed, cover, and chill in the refrigerator until ready to serve. You can make this up to 2 days ahead.

Cucumber Salad

This cool, refreshing salad is ideal with spicy grilled meats.

    1/4 cup rice vinegar
    1 teaspoon sugar
    1 tablespoon soy sauce
    1 teaspoon Asian sesame oil
    2 large cucumbers, peeled, halved lengthwise, and thinly sliced

Combine the vinegar and sugar in a medium bowl or pot, and stir until the sugar is dissolved. Stir in the soy sauce and sesame oil. Toss the cucumber slices with the dressing, and let stand 5 minutes before serving.

Serves 4

MAKE IT AT HOME

Prepare as directed. Refrigerate until ready to serve. You can make this salad 1 day ahead and store it, covered, in the refrigerator.

Endive and Apple Salad with Blue Cheese

This classic combination of bitter greens, tart fruit, and salty cheese seems terribly sophisticated when you're devouring it at a picnic table under the stars.

  4 to 6 Belgian endives, sliced into 1/2-inch pieces
  I tart green apple (Granny Smith or Pippin), cored and sliced into thin wedges
  4 ounces crumbled blue cheese (about 1/2 cup)
  Basic Vinaigrette Dressing (see recipe, page 43), made with sherry vinegar or red wine vinegar

Mix all the ingredients in a medium bowl or pot until well combined. Serve immediately.

Serves 4

Variation:
For a more unusual salad, substitute 3 firm, ripe Fuyu persimmons—peeled, halved, and sliced into thin half-circles—for the apples.

MAKE IT AT HOME

Garnish with Candied Pecans for a special touch.

Candied Pecans

Preheat the oven to 375°F. Blanch 1 1/2 cups pecans in boiling water for 5 minutes, and drain well. Toss the nuts with 1/4 cup sugar and 1 teaspoon salt, and spread on a baking sheet. Toast in the oven, stirring occasionally, about 15 minutes, or until crunchy. Spread the nuts on waxed paper to cool. These can be made ahead and stored in an airtight container for several weeks.

Lemony Couscous Salad

Couscous is one of my favorite camping foods since it is so easy to cook—just add boiling water and let it sit for 5 minutes. Lemon zest adds citrusy oomph to this simple salad.

I cup water
I teaspoon salt
I cup couscous
Juice and zest of 2 lemons
I medium cucumber, peeled, seeded, and diced
I medium red, orange, or yellow bell pepper, seeded and diced
2 green onions, thinly sliced
2 tablespoons olive oil

Bring the water, with the salt added, to a boil in a saucepan on a camp stove. Remove from the heat, add the couscous, stir, and cover. Let sit for 5 minutes. Fluff with a fork and allow to cool. Stir in the remaining ingredients and serve.

Serves 4

MAKE IT AT HOME

Prepare as directed , boiling the water on the stove top. Cover and chill in the refrigerator until ready to serve. You can make this up to 2 days ahead.

Middle Eastern Salad

This colorful salad is a satisfying side dish for grilled fish, chicken, or lamb.

Juice of 2 lemons or ¼ cup red wine vinegar
1½ teaspoons salt
½ teaspoon pepper
1 small clove garlic, minced
⅓ cup olive oil
1 head romaine lettuce, shredded
¾ cup chopped fresh mint
1 medium cucumber, peeled, seeded, and diced
3 medium tomatoes, diced
3 green onions, thinly sliced

Mix the lemon juice or vinegar, salt, pepper, garlic, and olive oil in a large pot or bowl until well combined. Add the lettuce, mint, cucumber, tomato, and green onion, and toss until the vegetables are evenly coated with the dressing. Serve immediately.

Serves 4

Variation:
Top with 2 ounces of crumbled feta cheese and/or 2 tablespoons toasted pine nuts.

Olive, Orange, and Couscous Salad

This flavorful salad is a nice accompaniment for any grilled meat.

> 1 cup water
> 1 teaspoon salt
> 1 cup couscous
> Zest and chopped segments of 1 orange
> 1/2 cup chopped, pitted cured olives, such as kalamata
> 2 green onions, thinly sliced
> 2 tablespoons olive oil
> Juice of 2 lemons
> Salt and pepper
> 4 ounces feta cheese, crumbled (about 1/2 cup)

Bring the water, with the salt added, to a boil in a saucepan with a lid on a camp stove. Remove from the heat; add the couscous, stir, and cover. Let sit for 5 minutes. Fluff with a fork and allow to cool. Mix in the orange zest and segments, olives, green onion, olive oil, lemon juice, salt, pepper, and feta. Serve immediately.

Serves 4

MAKE IT AT HOME

Prepare as directed, boiling the water on the stove top. Cover and chill in the refrigerator until ready to serve. You can make this up to 2 days ahead.

Thai Cabbage Salad

This salad is a perfect accompaniment for Chicken Skewers with Spicy Peanut Sauce (see recipe, page 135).

> 1 small head napa cabbage, finely shredded
> 1/2 small red onion, thinly sliced
> 1/4 cup chopped fresh mint leaves
> 1 large carrot, grated
> Juice of 2 limes
> 2 tablespoons Thai fish sauce (soy sauce may be substituted)
> 1 teaspoon sugar
> 1 serrano or jalapeño chile, seeded and finely chopped

MAKE IT AT HOME

Prepare as directed, cover, and store in the refrigerator until ready to serve. You can make this up to 1 day ahead.

Mix the cabbage, onion, mint, and carrot in a large bowl or pot until well combined. Mix the lime juice, fish or soy sauce, sugar, and chile in a separate bowl until well combined. Toss with the cabbage mixture and serve.

Serves 4

* Recipe is vegetarian if prepared with soy sauce instead of fish sauce.

White Bean and Roasted Garlic Salad with Grilled Zucchini

This hearty salad, served with crusty bread, is a filling vegetarian meal for a warm summer night. It is also a nice side dish to accompany grilled chicken or smoked sausages.

4 medium zucchini
Olive oil spray or nonstick cooking spray
Salt and pepper
1 small red onion, chopped
2 15-ounce cans white beans, drained and rinsed
6 cloves Roasted Garlic (see recipe, page 110), minced
Basic Vinaigrette Dressing (see recipe, page 43), made with balsamic vinegar
4 ounces feta or goat cheese, crumbled (about 1/2 cup, optional)

MAKE IT AT HOME

Slice the zucchini in half lengthwise, spray with olive oil spray, and roast in a hot oven (425°F), turning once during cooking, about 20 minutes, until cooked through. Continue with preparation as directed. Cover and chill until ready to serve. Top with crumbled feta or goat cheese, if using, just before serving. You can make this salad up to 2 days ahead.

Slice the zucchini in half lengthwise, spray with olive oil spray, sprinkle with salt and pepper to taste, and grill over hot coals for 5 to 7 minutes per side, until cooked through. Remove from the grill, allow to cool, and chop into 1/2-inch dice.

Place the beans in a large bowl. Add the grilled zucchini, roasted garlic, and red onion, and stir to combine.

Toss the beans and vegetables with the dressing. Serve topped with the crumbled feta or goat cheese, if using.

Serves 4

Grilled Vegetable Salad with Goat Cheese

Fire-roasted vegetables give this salad a smoky complexity. Sweet balsamic vinaigrette and creamy goat cheese balance out the flavors nicely.

Olive oil spray or nonstick cooking spray
2 small heads radicchio, halved
2 medium yellow crookneck squash, halved lengthwise
2 medium zucchini, halved lengthwise
1 large red onion, cut into 1/2-inch-thick slices
Salt and pepper
4 cups mixed greens
Basic Vinaigrette Dressing (see recipe, page 43), made with balsamic vinegar
4 ounces goat cheese, crumbled (about 1/2 cup)

> ### MAKE IT AT HOME
>
> Preheat the oven to 450°F. Halve, spray, and season the vegetables as directed. Place the vegetables in a single layer, cut sides down, and roast in the oven, turning once, 20 to 25 minutes, until tender. Remove the vegetables from the oven, cool, dice, and toss with the greens. Toss with the vinaigrette and top with the cheese.

Spray olive oil on the radicchio, yellow squash, zucchini, and onion slices. Season with salt and pepper. Place the vegetables on the grill over medium-high heat. Grill the vegetables, turning once, 10 to 15 minutes, until tender. Remove each vegetable from the grill as it is cooked. Let cool.

Dice the grilled vegetables and toss with the greens in a large bowl or pot. Pour the vinaigrette over all and toss to coat. Top with the crumbled cheese and serve.

Serves 4

CHAPTER 9

MIDAFTERNOON MUNCHIES: SNACKS AND APPETIZERS

Late afternoons and early evenings, when you've returned to camp after a day of hiking, rafting, swimming, or otherwise working up an appetite, you'll be ready to relax. A tasty snack (along with a nice cold beer!) is just the thing to take the edge off while you muster up the energy to get started on dinner preparations. The recipes in this chapter fit the bill, and many can also do double duty as side dishes for the evening's meal.

Simply Perfect Guacamole

My mother taught me to make this guacamole when I was a kid, and all my life I've been amazed by the extremes to which people will go to ruin a perfectly good avocado. As far as I'm concerned, things like mayonnaise, sour cream, and garlic have no place in guacamole. A little chopped tomato or onion, fine, but let's just leave it at that.

Be sure to use Hass avocados (the kind with bumpy black skin), as they have the best flavor and texture.

   2 medium Hass avocados, peeled, pitted, and chopped
   ½ teaspoon salt
   Juice of ½ lime
   2 to 3 tablespoons spicy store-bought tomato salsa or homemade
      salsa (see pages 104–105)

Smash the avocados with a fork, in a medium bowl, until only a few lumps remain. Mix in the salt, lime juice, and salsa. Taste for seasoning, and serve immediately.

Serves 4

Salsas

CHOPPED TOMATO SALSA 🫑 🔥

Use this fresh, spicy salsa to top Grilled Steak Tacos (see recipe, page 151) or as a dip for tortilla chips.

    I small red onion, chopped
    1/2 teaspoon salt
    Juice of 2 limes
    4 red or green jalapeño chiles, seeded and finely chopped
    4 medium tomatoes, chopped
    I cup chopped cilantro

Place the chopped onion in a bowl, sprinkle with the salt, squeeze the lime juice over, and set aside for 15 to 20 minutes. Add the chopped chiles, tomatoes, and cilantro to the onion mixture, and stir. Serve immediately.

Makes about 2 cups

Variation:
Tomato and Corn Salsa Add I cup fresh or frozen (thawed) corn kernels along with the chopped chile, tomato, and cilantro.

TROPICAL FRUIT SALSA 🫑 🔥

This fruity salsa is especially pretty made with a mix of green and red chiles. Serve it with tacos or with grilled salmon or steak.

    2 to 4 green and red jalapeño chiles, seeded and chopped
    Juice of I lime
    I1/2 cups chopped pineapple (canned, unsweetened is fine), mango,
      papaya, or a combination
    1/2 teaspoon salt

Mix all the ingredients until well combined, and serve.

Makes about 2 cups

FIRE-ROASTED SALSA 🫑 🔥

Roasting the vegetables over the fire gives this salsa a deep, smoky flavor. Try it with everything from tortilla chips to scrambled eggs, quesadillas, and tacos.

8 to 10 medium tomatoes
2 to 4 fresh serrano or jalapeño chiles, or to taste
1 small onion, peeled and cut into 1/2-inch-thick slices
1/2 cup chopped fresh cilantro
1 teaspoon salt
2 teaspoons wine vinegar

Place the tomatoes, chiles, and onion slices on the grill over high heat. Cook about 5 minutes, until the onion slices soften and begin to brown and the skins of the tomatoes and chiles begin to blacken and blister in spots. Turn the vegetables and continue cooking about 5 minutes more, until they are charred all over. As the vegetables are cooked, set them aside to cool.

When the vegetables are cool enough to handle, skin and chop the tomatoes. Remove the stems, skins, and seeds from the chiles. Chop the chiles and onion, and add them, along with the chopped tomato, to a medium bowl or pot. Stir in the cilantro, salt, and vinegar. Serve immediately, or cover and store in a cooler up to 3 days.

Makes about 2 1/2 cups

MAKE IT AT HOME

Preheat the broiler. Roast the tomatoes, chiles, and onion slices as in the recipe. Continue with recipe as directed, but purée the vegetables in a blender or food processor before adding the cilantro. You can make this up to 3 days ahead and store it, covered, in the refrigerator.

Smoked Salmon Crostini

Most commonly used as a condiment for sushi, wasabi* adds a surprising kick to these canapés. Prepared horseradish would be a fine substitute.

    1/2 baguette, cut into 1/2-inch-thick slices
    Olive oil spray or nonstick cooking spray
    1 to 2 tablespoons prepared wasabi paste
    3 ounces thinly sliced smoked salmon
    3 green onions, thinly sliced, or 2 tablespoons chopped chives

Spray the bread slices on both sides with olive oil spray. Grill over medium-high heat until browned on both sides. Spread each slice with a bit of wasabi, top with a slice of salmon, and sprinkle with green onion or chive. Serve immediately.

Serves 4

* This spicy Japanese horseradish is available in the Asian food section of most supermarkets.

MAKE IT AT HOME

Toast the bread in a toaster oven or under the broiler. Proceed with preparation as directed.

Pear and Prosciutto Bruschetta with Balsamic Syrup

If you don't have pears, many other fruits can be substituted. Melon is a classic partner for prosciutto, or you could use apples, figs, or even peaches or apricots.

Olive oil spray or nonstick cooking spray
8 thin slices crusty French or Italian bread
4 ounces Gorgonzola cheese or goat cheese (about $1/2$ cup, optional)
2 large, ripe pears, cored and sliced about $1/8$ inch thick
8 paper-thin slices prosciutto
Balsamic Syrup (see recipe, page 51)
Pepper

Spray the bread on both sides with olive oil. Toast on a grill, turning once, 2 to 3 minutes per side, until both sides are golden brown. Top each piece of bread with a little cheese (if using), a couple of slices of pear, and a slice of prosciutto. Drizzle with Balsamic Syrup, sprinkle with pepper, and serve.

Serves 4

MAKE IT AT HOME

Toast the bread in a toaster oven or under the broiler. Proceed with preparation as directed.

Savory Cheese S'mores

Made just like the dessert version, this is a fun snack for children and adults alike. These treats are best made over a fire, one at a time, so that you can slide the gooey cheese onto a cracker and right into your mouth.

    32 crackers, preferably whole wheat

    1/4 cup purchased sun-dried tomato pesto or olive tapenade

    16 fresh basil leaves (optional)

    16 bocconcini* or any firm cheese cut into 16 1-inch cubes

For each s'more, set out two crackers and spread one with about 1 teaspoon of pesto or olive spread. Top with a basil leaf, if using. Spear a cheese ball or cube on a long stick or skewer. If using fresh mozzarella, squeeze the cheese with a paper towel to remove excess water. Hold the skewered cheese over an open fire or very hot coals. Cook for about 2 minutes, turning the skewer to melt and brown the cheese evenly on all sides. Using the dry cracker, a fork, or a knife, scrape the cheese onto the cracker with the spread and basil leaf. Top with the second cracker to make a sandwich. Eat immediately.

Makes 16 sandwiches (serves 4 to 6 as an appetizer)

* Bocconcini are small balls of fresh mozzarella. If they are unavailable, cut 8 ounces fresh mozzarella into 1-inch cubes.

MAKE IT AT HOME

Try Oven-Baked Mozzarella Canapés instead.

Oven-Baked Mozzarella Canapés

Preheat the oven to 400°F. Use 16 thin slices of baguette in place of the crackers. Top each baguette slice with a bit of pesto or tapenade, then a slice of mozzarella. Cook in the oven 8 to 10 minutes, until the bread is crisp and the cheese is melted. If desired, finish under the broiler for a golden top. Garnish with shredded fresh basil.

Bacon-Wrapped Grilled Figs

When I was growing up, the only figs I knew were smooshed between the cakey layers of Fig Newtons. A dream opened my eyes to the allure of this mysteriously exotic fruit: Biting into one of the ripe orbs, sweet juice filled my mouth, quickly followed by the satisfying crunch of seeds between my teeth.

When I told my friends about the dream, they laughed. It was just about sex, they said, classic Freudian imagery. Figs are a sexy fruit.

But my dream didn't fill me with carnal urges. It just made me want to eat a fig. A fresh, ripe, sumptuous, juicy fig. In this deceptively simple recipe, crisp, salty bacon highlights the complex sweetness of the figs in an ideal marriage of flavors and textures.

> **MAKE IT AT HOME**
>
> Preheat the oven to 475°F. Wrap each fig in bacon and secure with a tooth-pick. Place on a baking sheet and cook, turning occasionally, about 10 minutes, until the bacon is crisp.

12 small fresh, ripe figs
6 slices bacon, cut in half

Wrap each fig with half a slice of bacon. Thread a skewer through 3 of the wrapped figs (the skewer should go through the bacon to hold it in place), leaving a bit of space between the figs. To make it easier to turn the skewers, thread a second skewer through the figs, parallel to the first, about 1/4 inch apart. Repeat with the rest of the figs. Cook on a grill over high heat, turning frequently, about 6 to 8 minutes, until the bacon is crisp. Serve hot.

Serves 4

Roasted Garlic

Roasting garlic brings out all its sweetness. Spread the soft cloves on slices of toasted baguette.

    1 large head garlic
    1 tablespoon olive oil

Slice the top off the head of garlic, exposing the tops of the cloves. Place the garlic head on a square of aluminum foil and drizzle with the olive oil. Wrap the garlic tightly in the foil, and place directly on hot coals. Cook about 30 minutes, until the cloves are soft. Remove from the fire with tongs. Unwrap the garlic and serve. Individual cloves can be squeezed out and spread on toast.

Serves 4

MAKE IT AT HOME

Preheat the oven to 450°F. Prepare the garlic as directed. Roast in the oven about 45 minutes, until soft. Serve as directed.

Parmesan Baked Apples

Sweet apples, such as Macintosh or Gala, provide a nice counterpoint to the salty cheese, but tart Granny Smith or Pippin apples will work as well. Serve the baked apples with slices of crusty bread as a snack or appetizer or as an accompaniment to grilled pork or duck breast.

Olive oil spray or nonstick cooking spray

2 large apples, peeled, quartered, cored, and cut into 1/4-inch-thick slices

4 ounces good-quality Parmesan cheese, thinly sliced (use a vegetable peeler to get paper-thin slices of cheese)

Prepare 4 squares of aluminum foil by spraying with olive oil or nonstick cooking spray. Place one-eighth of the apple slices on each square of foil in a single layer, and top with one-eighth (about 1/2 ounce) of the cheese. Repeat with another layer of apple slices and cheese for each packet. Wrap up the foil, leaving room in each packet for heat and steam to circulate. Cook on a grill over high heat, 10 to 12 minutes, until the apple slices are soft. To serve, slide the apples onto plates and drizzle with the syrupy juice that has accumulated in each packet.

Serves 4

Variation:

Top the apple slices and cheese in each packet with 1 ounce of thinly sliced dry salami (4 ounces total) before cooking.

MAKE IT AT HOME

Preheat the oven to 450°F. Bake the apples in individual ramekins, covered with foil, for 8 to 10 minutes, until the apple slices are soft. Uncover and finish under the broiler for a crisp, golden crust.

Indonesian Peanut Dip

Spicy and sweet, this dip is perfect for scooping up with raw or steamed vegetables. Bell peppers, broccoli, cauliflower, carrots, cucumbers, and green beans are all good choices. It is also delicious thinned with a little extra lemon juice and tossed with a salad of lettuce, cucumbers, and shredded carrots.

$^1/_2$ cup water

I cup peanut butter (preferably crunchy)

$^1/_4$ cup soy sauce

$^1/_4$ cup packed brown sugar

I to 2 teaspoons crushed red pepper, or to taste

2 tablespoons bottled chili sauce or ketchup

Juice of I lemon

MAKE IT AT HOME

Prepare as directed above. You can make this dip up to 1 week ahead and keep it, covered, in the refrigerator or cooler. Bring to room temperature before serving.

Mix all the ingredients in a small bowl or saucepan until well combined. Serve immediately, or cover and chill for up to I week. Bring to room temperature before serving.

Makes about 2 cups

Baba Ghanoush
(Middle Eastern Eggplant Spread)

This tangy, smoky dip is a snap to make and will keep, in a tightly sealed container in a cooler, for several days. Served with some olives and warm pita for dipping, it makes a great snack. Add a Middle Eastern Salad (see recipe, page 97) and some purchased hummus to make it a meal.

2 large eggplants
2 tablespoons olive oil
1/3 cup tahini*
Juice of 2 lemons
1 clove garlic, minced
1 teaspoon salt
1 teaspoon ground cumin
1/4 to 1/2 teaspoon cayenne (optional)
Pita rounds for serving

MAKE IT AT HOME

Preheat the broiler. Cut the eggplants in half lengthwise, and place, cut-side down, on a baking sheet. Cook under the broiler 15 to 20 minutes, until the skin blackens and the flesh is soft. Mince the garlic in a food processor. Add the remaining ingredients, including the eggplant flesh, and process until smooth.

Prick the whole eggplants with a fork. Roast over hot coals or open flames 10 to 15 minutes, until soft and charred (charring the skin—which is removed after cooking—gives the dish its characteristic smoky flavor). Allow to cool. Then either pull the charred skin off the eggplants or halve them and scoop out the flesh with a spoon. Discard the skin. Mince the eggplant flesh. Mix the eggplant, olive oil, tahini, lemon juice, garlic, salt, cumin, and cayenne in a medium bowl or pot until well combined. Warm the pita rounds over the fire or hot coals, slice into wedges, and serve alongside the dip.

Makes about 2 cups

* Tahini is a Middle Eastern sesame paste available in specialty food stores or the ethnic food aisle of many supermarkets.

DINNER'S ON: ENTRÉES

As the sun goes down, the woods get quiet, and the crisp chill of the outdoors begins to settle in for the night. There's just no better way to spend this magical time than sharing a delicious meal with your companions around a crackling fire. Following are recipes to suit just about any mood or taste—from spicy and exotic dishes to comfort foods that'll warm your soul.

Burgers

Burgers—whether made from ground turkey, beef, lamb, or mushrooms—are among the best camping foods around. They're easy to prepare, and virtually everyone loves some version of them.

The biggest mistake people make when cooking burgers is to press down on them with the spatula as they cook. I know it's tempting to hear the sizzle of the juice hitting the fire, but when you squeeze out the juice, you lose much of the flavor and can make your burgers turn out dry. For the tastiest, juiciest burgers, just let them be.

Toast the hamburger buns while the burgers are cooking. Choose from many possible garnishes:

Lettuce
Thinly sliced tomato
Thinly sliced onion
Thinly sliced avocado
Ketchup
Mustard (whole grain, Dijon, honey, etc.)
Relish
Mayonnaise
Chili sauce
Basic Barbecue Spice Rub (see recipe, page 48) or purchased barbecue sauce
Cilantro
Any cheese (cheddar, goat, feta, blue, Swiss, etc.)
Aioli (see recipes, pages 63–65)
Simply Perfect Guacamole (see recipe, page 103)
Chopped Tomato Salsa (see recipe, page 104), Fire-Roasted Salsa (see recipe, page 105), or purchased salsa
Spicy Peanut Sauce (see recipe, page 56) or Indonesian Peanut Dip (see recipe, page 112)
Yogurt Mint Sauce (see recipe, page 57)

MAKE IT AT HOME

If you don't have an outdoor grill on which to make great burgers, prepare the meat mixture as directed in the recipes. Then cook in a ridged grill pan or skillet on a stove top over medium-high heat, or under a broiler, about 4 minutes per side, until cooked to desired doneness.

CHIPOTLE TURKEY BURGERS

Garnish these smoky-spicy burgers with Simply Perfect Guacamole
(see recipe, page 103), fresh cilantro, and a dollop of salsa. Black Bean
Salad (see recipe, page 92) or a crisp green salad with Citrus Salad
Dressing (see recipe, page 44) would be perfect accompaniments.

  1 1/4 pounds lean ground turkey
  1 egg, lightly beaten
  2 green onions, thinly sliced
  2 seeded, minced chipotle chiles from a can of chipotles in
    adobo,* plus 2 tablespoons of the sauce
  1 teaspoon ground cumin
  1 teaspoon salt
  1/2 teaspoon pepper
  4 ounces sharp cheddar cheese, thinly sliced or grated (about 1/2 cup)
  4 hamburger buns, toasted

Mix together the ground turkey, egg, onion, minced chipotles and
sauce, cumin, salt, and pepper in a medium bowl or pot until well
combined. Shape the mixture into 4 1-inch-thick patties.

Grill the burgers over medium-high heat about 5 minutes, until
browned on the bottom. Flip the burgers, top each with one-quarter
(about 1 ounce) of the cheese, and continue cooking about 5 minutes
more, until the burgers are cooked through and the cheese is melted.
Serve the burgers on toasted buns with desired garnishes.

Serves 4

* Chipotle chiles are smoked jalapeños, usually canned in adobo sauce. Find them
  in Latin American food stores or the ethnic food aisle of many supermarkets.

SOUTHEAST ASIAN TURKEY BURGERS

Fresh herbs give these burgers an exotic twist. Serve them garnished
with Spicy Peanut Sauce (see recipe, page 56) and accompanied by
Cucumber Salad (see recipe, page 94) for a special treat.

1¼ pounds lean ground turkey
1 egg, lightly beaten
2 cloves garlic, minced
⅓ cup packed chopped fresh cilantro leaves
⅓ cup packed chopped fresh basil leaves
⅓ cup packed chopped fresh mint leaves
Juice of 2 limes
2 teaspoons sugar
1 jalapeño chile, seeded and minced
1 teaspoon salt
4 hamburger buns, toasted

Mix the ground turkey, egg, garlic, cilantro, basil, mint, lime juice, sugar, chile, and salt in a medium bowl or pot until well combined. Form the mixture into 4 1-inch-thick patties. Grill the burgers over medium-high heat, 6 to 8 minutes per side, until browned and cooked through. Serve the burgers on toasted buns with desired garnishes.

Serves 4

SUN-DRIED TOMATO AND BASIL BURGERS

A little Dijon mustard and lettuce are all these flavorful burgers need.

1¼ pounds lean ground beef
1 egg, lightly beaten
2 cloves garlic, minced
3 tablespoons chopped fresh basil
3 tablespoons drained and chopped oil-cured sun-dried tomatoes
1 teaspoon salt
1 teaspoon pepper
4 hamburger buns, toasted

Mix the meat, egg, garlic, basil, sun-dried tomatoes, salt, and pepper in a medium bowl or pot until well combined. Form the mixture into 4 1-inch-thick patties.

Grill the burgers over medium-high heat, about 4 minutes per side, until cooked to desired doneness. (If you're using ground turkey instead of ground beef, be sure the burgers are cooked through completely, with no pink in the middle.) Serve the burgers on toasted buns with desired garnishes.

Serves 4

Variation:
Top each burger with 1 1/2 ounces soft, fresh goat cheese about 2 minutes before removing it from the grill.

BLUE CHEESE MUSHROOM BURGERS

Serve these tasty burgers on whole wheat buns with just a touch of mayonnaise and some crisp lettuce.

 1 1/4 pounds lean ground beef
 1 egg, lightly beaten
 1/2 cup finely chopped fresh mushrooms
 1 small red onion, finely chopped
 1/4 cup Worcestershire sauce
 1/2 teaspoon salt
 1/2 teaspoon pepper
 4 ounces blue cheese, crumbled (about 1/2 cup)
 4 hamburger buns, toasted

Mix the ground beef, egg, mushrooms, onion, Worcestershire sauce, salt, and pepper in a medium bowl or pot until well combined. Form the mixture into 4 1-inch-thick patties.

Grill the burgers over medium-high heat, about 4 minutes, until the bottom is browned. Flip the burgers, top each with one-quarter (about 1 ounce) of the cheese, and continue cooking, about 4 minutes more, until the cheese is melted and the burgers are cooked to desired doneness. Serve the burgers on toasted buns with desired garnishes.

Serves 4

CHEDDAR-STUFFED BURGERS

I like these cheeseburgers on a toasted bun with a bit of spicy barbecue sauce, thin slices of red onion and tomato, and a bit of crisp lettuce. Serve with a green salad or Creole Slaw (see recipe, page 93).

   1 1/4 pound lean ground beef
   1 egg, lightly beaten
   1 small red onion, finely chopped
   3 tablespoons Worcestershire sauce
   1/2 teaspoon salt
   1/2 teaspoon pepper
   4 ounces grated sharp cheddar cheese (about 1/2 cup)
   4 hamburger buns, toasted

Mix the ground beef, egg, onion, Worcestershire sauce, salt, and pepper in a medium bowl or pot until well combined. Form the mixture into 8 thin patties. Top 4 of the patties with 1/4 cup each of the grated cheese, then top with another patty and seal shut.

   Grill the burgers over medium-high heat, about 4 minutes per side, until cooked to the desired doneness. Serve the burgers on toasted buns with desired garnishes.

Serves 4

GREEK LAMB BURGERS

Stuff these tangy burgers into pita and top with shredded lettuce and Yogurt Mint Sauce (see recipe, page 57).

   1 1/4 pounds ground lamb
   1 egg, lightly beaten
   1 teaspoon cumin
   2 tablespoons chopped fresh mint leaves
   1 teaspoon grated lemon zest
   1 teaspoon salt
   1/2 teaspoon pepper
   4 hamburger buns, toasted

Mix the lamb, egg, cumin, mint, zest, salt, and pepper in a medium bowl or pot until well combined. Form the mixture into 4 1-inch-thick patties. Grill over hot coals, about 5 minutes per side, until cooked to the desired doneness. Serve the burgers on toasted buns with desired garnishes.

Serves 4

GRILLED PORTOBELLO BURGERS WITH OLIVE AIOLI

These "burgers" garnished with a flavorful aioli are a great vegetarian alternative to hamburgers.

4 large portobello mushrooms, stems trimmed
Olive oil spray or nonstick cooking spary
Salt and pepper
4 hamburger buns, toasted
Olive Aioli (see recipe, page 65)
1/2 cup purchased roasted red bell peppers

Spray the mushrooms all over with olive oil. Season with salt and pepper to taste. Grill over medium-high heat, 7 to 8 minutes per side, until tender. Serve the "burgers" on toasted buns spread with Olive Aioli and topped with roasted peppers and any other desired garnishes.

Serves 4

San Francisco Cioppino

Cioppino is a rich, tomatoey seafood stew that originated in my home-town of San Francisco. Dungeness crab is a staple of true San Francisco cioppino, but you can use any combination of fish and shellfish. Cod, bass, and snapper are good mild-flavored fishes for this stew. Shrimp (peeled), squid, and scallops are nice hearty additions, and clams and mussels in their shells make for a dramatic presentation. Out in the wild, I like to use frozen cod and a bag of frozen mixed seafood. Serve with Neoclassic Garlic Aioli (see recipe, page 63), crusty sourdough bread, and a crisp green salad.

2 tablespoons olive oil
4 cloves garlic, minced
1 medium onion, diced
2 teaspoons dried oregano
$^1/_2$ to 1 teaspoon crushed red pepper flakes
$1^1/_2$ teaspoons salt
1 teaspoon pepper
$1^1/_2$ cups dry red wine
2 14-ounce cans tomato purée
3 14-ounce cans chicken broth
$2^1/_2$ pounds (total) fish (chopped into
 2-inch pieces) and shellfish

MAKE IT AT HOME

Prepare as directed and garnish with garlic croutons. Drop a couple of croutons into each bowl of stew or serve them alongside.

Heat the oil in a large pot over medium-high heat on a camp stove. Add the garlic and onion, and cook, stirring, until the onion is soft and translucent, about 5 minutes. Add the oregano, red pepper, salt, and pepper. Add the wine and cook, about 10 minutes, until reduced by half. Add the tomato purée and broth, cover, and simmer about 30 minutes.

Just before serving, bring the broth to a boil. Add the fish and shell-fish and simmer, about 7 minutes, until the shells (if using clams or mussels in their shells) open (discarding any that don't open) and all the seafood is cooked through. Serve immediately.

Serves 4

Lemon Garlic Shrimp

Pack frozen shrimp in your cooler, and plan to eat it on the second day of your trip. The frozen shrimp will help keep your cooler cold. Serve crusty grilled bread or garlic bread alongside for soaking up the tangy sauce. Alternatively, you could toss the cooked shrimp and the sauce from the packets with hot, cooked pasta.

Olive oil spray or nonstick cooking spray
Juice and zest of 1 lemon
1/2 cup white wine
3 cloves garlic, minced
1/4 cup minced flat-leaf parsley
1/2 teaspoon salt
1/2 teaspoon pepper
2 pounds shrimp, peeled
3 tablespoons butter, cut into pieces

MAKE IT AT HOME

Preheat the oven to 400°F. Place the shrimp in a baking dish. Mix all the other ingredients, except the butter, and pour over the shrimp. Top with the butter, cover with foil, and bake, stirring occasionally, about 20 minutes, until the shrimp are cooked through.

Prepare 4 squares of aluminum foil by spraying with oil. Mix the lemon juice and zest, wine, garlic, parsley, salt, and pepper in a medium bowl or pot until well combined. Toss with the shrimp. Place one-quarter (about 1/2 pound) of the shrimp in the center of each piece of foil. Fold up the sides of the foil, top with the butter pieces, and drizzle about 1 tablespoon of the marinade over each pile of shrimp. Fold the edges of the foil together to form a tightly sealed packet, leaving space for heat and steam to circulate inside. Grill the packets over high heat, 15 to 20 minutes, until the shrimp are cooked through. Serve immediately in packets to maintain a nice pool of sauce for dipping.

Serves 4

Coconut Shrimp

This Latin American–inspired dish has a spicy kick that makes it perfect for a cold night by the fire. Serve it over rice—and be sure to include the rich coconut milk sauce.

Juice of 2 limes
1 14-ounce can diced tomatoes, drained
1 14-ounce can light unsweetened coconut milk
2 jalapeño or serrano chiles, halved, seeded, and sliced
1 teaspoon salt
2 pounds shrimp, peeled
2 cups green beans, cut into 1-inch pieces
Olive oil spray or nonstick cooking spray

Mix the lime juice, tomatoes, coconut milk, chile slices, and salt in a medium bowl or pot until well combined. Toss with the shrimp and green bean pieces. Prepare 4 large squares of aluminum foil by spraying with olive oil or cooking spray. Place one-quarter of the shrimp mixture in the center of each foil square, fold up the sides, and spoon some of the coconut milk mixture remaining in the bowl over each. Seal securely, leaving room for heat and steam to circulate inside.

Grill the packets over high heat, 15 to 20 minutes, until the shrimp are cooked through. Serve immediately.

Serves 4

MAKE IT AT HOME

Mix the chile slices, lime juice, tomatoes, and coconut milk in a large pot on the stove top until well combined. Bring to a boil and add the green bean pieces, shrimp, and salt. Simmer, about 15 minutes, until the shrimp are cooked through. Serve immediately.

Spicy Creole Shrimp

The sauce is where all the flavor of this dish is, so serve it over rice or with crusty bread for sopping.

I large clove garlic, minced
I small onion, diced
I large red bell pepper, seeded and diced
I teaspoon paprika
I tablespoon chopped fresh thyme or I teaspoon dried thyme
1/8 to 1/2 teaspoon cayenne
1/2 teaspoon salt
1/2 teaspoon pepper
3 tablespoons Worcestershire sauce
Juice of I lemon
2 pounds shrimp, peeled
Olive oil spray or nonstick cooking spray
1/4 cup butter (1/2 stick), cut into pieces

MAKE IT AT HOME

Preheat the oven to 450°F. Prepare the shrimp mixture as directed and place in an 8- or 10-inch-square baking dish. Dot with the butter, cover with foil, and bake, stirring once or twice, 20 to 25 minutes, until the shrimp are cooked through.

Mix the garlic, onion, bell pepper, paprika, thyme, cayenne, salt, pepper, Worcestershire sauce, and lemon juice in a medium bowl or pot until well combined. Toss with the shrimp. Prepare 4 large squares of aluminum foil by spraying with olive oil or cooking spray.

Place one-quarter of the shrimp mixture in the center of each piece of foil, and top each with one-quarter of the butter. Fold up the sides and seal securely, leaving room for heat and steam to circulate inside.

Grill the packets over high heat, 15 to 20 minutes, until the shrimp are cooked through. Serve immediately.

Serves 4

Grilled Prawns with Hoisin Glaze

Make it easy to turn the skewers on the grill by threading 2 bamboo skewers through the prawns (the skewers should be parallel to each other, about $1/4$ inch apart), which keeps the prawns from spinning when you lift the skewers.

  2 pounds prawns, peeled
  Juice of 2 limes
  1 tablespoon peeled and chopped fresh ginger
  Salt and pepper
  Hoisin Glaze (see recipe, page 54)

Thread the shrimp onto the skewers, and squeeze the lime juice over them. Sprinkle with the ginger, and season with salt and pepper.

  Cook the shrimp over a hot fire, about 3 minutes per side, until cooked through. Baste with Hoisin Glaze and serve.

Serves 4

MAKE IT AT HOME

Spread the shrimp in a single layer on a baking sheet, squeeze the lime juice over them, sprinkle with the ginger, and season with salt and pepper. Broil, 2 to 3 minutes, until cooked through. Baste with Hoisin Glaze; serve hot.

Shrimp and Noodles in Peanut Sauce

Cooking green beans and shrimp along with the pasta in a large pot of water makes this dish a cinch to prepare—and to clean up. Add variety with different vegetables—try carrots, snow peas, or broccoli. Or substitute cooked chicken or tofu (tossed in with the sauce) for the shrimp.

    Salt
    12 ounces soba* or spaghetti noodles
    12 ounces green beans, trimmed and cut into 1-inch pieces
    12 ounces shrimp, peeled
    Spicy Peanut Sauce (see recipe, page 56)

Bring 3 quarts of salted water to a boil in a large pot on a camp stove. Add the noodles. When the water returns to the boil, add the green beans. Continue to cook about 6 minutes, then add the shrimp. Cook, 2 to 3 minutes more, until the pasta is tender and the shrimp are pink. Drain the noodle mixture, and return to the pot. Toss with the peanut sauce and serve immediately.

Serves 4

* These Japanese buckwheat noodles are available in Asian markets and the Asian food section of many supermarkets.

MAKE IT AT HOME

This is a fast and easy dish for weeknight dinners—and the leftovers are great to take to work for lunch the next day. Prepare on the stove top as directed. The peanut sauce can be made up to 1 week ahead and stored, covered, in the refrigerator. Bring to room temperature before using.

Halibut with Fennel and Olives

Fresh fennel balances the strong salty flavor of the olives and keeps the fish moist while it cooks. Use only the bulb of the fennel, discarding the leafy tops.

2 tablespoons olive oil
$^2/_3$ cup chopped pitted kalamata olives
2 tablespoons drained bottled capers
1 large garlic clove, minced
1 tablespoon chopped fresh thyme or 1 teaspoon crumbled dried thyme
$^1/_4$ to $^1/_2$ teaspoon crushed red pepper flakes (optional)
Olive oil or nonstick cooking spray
1 medium fennel bulb, very thinly sliced
4 halibut fillets, about 6 ounces each
$^1/_4$ cup white wine

Mix the olive oil, chopped olive, capers, garlic, thyme, and red pepper (if using) in a small bowl or saucepan until well combined.

Prepare 4 squares of aluminum foil by spraying with olive oil or cooking spray. Place several slices of the fennel in the center of each foil square, and top with a halibut fillet. Spoon one-quarter of the olive mixture over each fish fillet, and fold up the sides of the foil squares. Drizzle one-quarter (1 tablespoon) of the wine over each fillet, and seal the foil packets, leaving room for heat and steam to circulate inside. Grill over high heat, 15 to 20 minutes, depending on the thickness of the fish, until cooked through. Serve immediately.

MAKE IT AT HOME

Preheat the oven to 400°F. Prepare the olive mixture as directed. Place the fennel slices in the bottom of an oiled baking dish large enough to hold the fish fillets in a single layer. Place the fish fillets on top of the fennel slices, then top with the olive mixture, dividing it equally among the fillets. Pour the wine over the fish. Cover the dish with foil and bake, 12 to 15 minutes, until the fish is cooked through. Serve immediately.

Serves 4

Fish Cooked with Curried Couscous

Any type of firm fish works well in this dish—salmon, cod, halibut, sea bass, or even shrimp or scallops. It's so easy to prepare and so flavorful that this dish will likely become one of the mainstays of your camping cuisine.

Olive oil spray or non-stick cooking spray
2/3 cup uncooked couscous
3 green onions, thinly sliced
1/2 cup slivered almonds
1/2 cup raisins
2 teaspoons curry powder
1/2 teaspoon cayenne
1 teaspoon salt, plus more for seasoning
1 1/2 cups chicken broth, divided (water may be substituted)
4 6-ounce cod or salmon fillets or 1 1/2 pounds shrimp or scallops
1/4 cup butter (1/2 stick), cut into pieces

> ## MAKE IT AT HOME
>
> Preheat the oven to 400°F. Prepare the couscous as directed and spread it in the bottom of an oiled glass baking dish large enough to hold the fish in a single layer. Lay the fish or seafood on top of the couscous, top with butter, sprinkle with salt, and pour the remaining broth over the top. Cover the dish with foil, and bake, about 15 minutes, until the fish is cooked through.

Mix the couscous, green onion, almond slivers, raisins, curry powder, cayenne, and salt in a small bowl or pot until well combined. Stir in half (3/4 cup) the chicken broth.

Prepare 4 squares of aluminum foil by spraying with cooking oil. Place one-quarter of the couscous mixture on each sheet of foil, top with 1 fish fillet and butter, and sprinkle with salt.

Fold up the sides of the foil and pour one-quarter of the remaining chicken broth into each packet. Double-fold the top and sides of each packet, leaving a bit of room for heat and steam to circulate inside.

Grill the packets over high heat, about 15 minutes, until the fish is cooked through and the couscous is tender. Serve immediately.

Serves 4

Place dry ingredients on the foil, then fold up the sides and add the chicken broth. Fold over the sides of the foil and form into a packet. Place entire packet on the grill to cook.

Orange-Herb Salmon

Serve this salmon with Grilled Asparagus (see recipe, page 169) and couscous with grilled sweet onions for an elegant meal under the stars.

Olive oil spray or nonstick cooking spray
4 6-ounce salmon fillets
Salt and pepper
Juice and zest of 1 orange
1 teaspoon crushed red pepper (or to taste)
1 tablespoon fennel seeds, crushed (crush seeds in a plastic bag, using an unopened can)
1/4 cup (1/2 stick) butter, cut into pieces

Spray 4 squares of aluminum foil with olive oil or nonstick cooking spray. Place 1 salmon fillet on each foil square. Sprinkle the fish with salt, pepper, orange juice and zest, red pepper, and fennel seeds. Dot each fillet with butter. Bring the sides of the foil up around the fish and fold over to seal the packet tightly, leaving room for heat and steam to circulate inside. Cook on a grill over high heat, about 20 minutes, until the fish is just cooked through. Serve immediately.

Serves 4

MAKE IT AT HOME

Preheat the oven to 400°F. Place the salmon fillets in the bottom of an oiled baking dish large enough to hold them in a single layer. Sprinkle with the salt, pepper, orange zest and juice, red pepper, and fennel seeds. Dot each fillet with butter. Cover the dish with foil. Bake, 20 to 25 minutes, until the fish is cooked through. Serve immediately.

Grilled Salmon with Balsamic Fig Sauce

Some say figs are an aphrodisiac, and this is a surprising way to sneak them into a meal. If fresh figs are unavailable, dried figs, which will plump up in the sauce, are a fine substitute.

$1^{1}/2$ cups balsamic vinegar
16 to 20 ripe black figs or dried black figs, stemmed and coarsely chopped
4 6-ounce salmon fillets
Olive oil spray or nonstick cooking spray
Salt and pepper

Place the vinegar and figs in a saucepan over medium-high heat on a camp stove. Bring to a boil and cook, stirring occasionally, 15 to 20 minutes, until the figs start to break down and the sauce thickens and becomes syrupy.

MAKE IT AT HOME

Prepare as directed, cooking the salmon either in a ridged grill pan or under a broiler, and cooking the sauce on the stove top.

While the sauce is cooking, spray the salmon with oil, season with salt and pepper, and grill over medium-high heat, 3 to 5 minutes per side, until cooked through. (You may want to use a grill basket for this if your fillets are thin and delicate.) Serve topped with the sauce.

Serves 4

Bourbon-Glazed Chicken

This is the perfect excuse to bring along a bottle of bourbon for a late-night warm-up. You can substitute red wine, port, sherry, or balsamic vinegar for the bourbon. Or use flank or skirt steak instead of chicken. Serve alongside Lemony Couscous Salad (see recipe, page 96).

4 boneless, skinless chicken breast halves
1/3 cup bourbon
3 tablespoons brown sugar
2 tablespoons soy sauce
1 tablespoon sesame oil
1 clove garlic, chopped
Juice of 1/2 lemon
1/2 teaspoon salt
1/2 teaspoon pepper

Place the chicken breasts in a ziplock bag and pound to flatten (using the bottle of bourbon or the side of a can as a mallet) to about 1-inch thickness. Mix the bourbon, brown sugar, soy sauce, sesame oil, garlic, lemon juice, salt, and pepper in a small bowl or saucepan until well combined. Pour into the bag with the chicken. Seal the bag and place in a cooler to marinate at least 1 hour and up to 8 hours. When ready to cook, place the chicken on a grill over high heat, reserving the marinade, and grill, 5 to 7 minutes per side, until the chicken is cooked through.

MAKE IT AT HOME

Prepare as directed, and cook the chicken in a ridged grill pan or heavy skillet on a stove top over medium-high heat, 5 to 7 minutes per side, until the chicken is cooked through. While the chicken is cooking, prepare the marinade as directed. Spoon a little of the glaze over each chicken breast. Serve immediately.

While the chicken is cooking, pour the leftover marinade into a pot and bring to a boil on a camp stove. Boil the marinade for at least 5 minutes (since it had raw chicken in it, this step is essential for safety). Continue to boil until the sauce thickens. Spoon a little of the glaze over each chicken breast. Serve immediately.

Serves 4

Chicken and Dumplings

This hearty stew is always a welcome treat on a cold night in the woods.

2 tablespoons vegetable oil or olive oil

1 medium yellow onion, peeled and chopped

4 medium carrots, peeled and sliced
   into coins

4 celery ribs, sliced

1 tablespoon chopped fresh thyme
   or 1 teaspoon dried thyme

4 14-ounce cans chicken broth

1 tablespoon hot pepper sauce, or more
   to taste (optional)

Salt and pepper

1½ pounds boneless, skinless chicken (use
   a combination of white and dark meat)

2 cups (one recipe) Multipurpose Baking
   Mix (see recipe, page 35)

1 egg, lightly beaten

1¼ cups milk

MAKE IT AT HOME

Prepare as directed, cooking on a stove top. The stew can be prepared a day ahead. Prepare the dumpling batter shortly before serving. Bring the stew to a boil and drop the dumpling batter in, cover, and simmer about 10 minutes. Serve hot.

Heat the oil in a large pot over medium-high heat on a camp stove. Cook the onion in the oil, stirring frequently, about 4 minutes, until translucent. Add the carrot, celery, thyme, and broth. Bring to a boil, season with hot pepper sauce, salt, and pepper to taste, and add the chicken. Simmer, about 15 minutes, until the chicken is cooked through.

Meanwhile, prepare the dumpling batter by mixing the baking mix, egg, and milk into a smooth batter in a medium bowl or pot.

When the chicken is cooked through, remove it from the pot and set aside to cool. Continue simmering the stock. When the chicken is cool enough to handle, shred or dice it, and return it to the stock. Bring the stew to a boil, and drop in the dumpling batter in heaping spoonfuls. Cover the pot and simmer about 10 minutes more. Serve hot.

Serves 4 to 6

Chicken Skewers with Spicy Peanut Sauce

To save time at the campsite, the peanut sauce can be made and the chicken can be skewered and marinated at home. Use sturdy freezer bags to store the skewered chicken so the sharp ends don't poke through the plastic.

1½ pounds skinless, boneless chicken breasts, cut into 1-inch pieces
2 teaspoons peeled and minced fresh ginger
Juice of 2 limes
Salt and pepper
Spicy Peanut Sauce (see recipe, page 56)

Thread the chicken pieces onto bamboo skewers, leaving about 1 inch at one end. To make the skewers easier to handle on the grill, thread a second skewer through the same chicken pieces, parallel to the first. Place the skewers in a large ziplock bag (you may need to use more than one bag). Mix the ginger, lime juice, salt, and pepper in a small bowl or saucepan until well combined. Pour into the bag with the skewers (divide evenly if using more than one bag). Zip the bag and shake to make sure all the chicken is coated with the marinade. Put the bag in a cooler until ready to grill the chicken. Marinate the chicken for at least 1 hour and up to 24 hours.

Grill the chicken skewers over medium-high heat, 6 to 7 minutes per side, until cooked through. Serve with the peanut sauce on the side for dipping, or drizzle sauce over each skewer.

Serves 4

Variation:
Substitute shrimp or beef for the chicken, or add vegetables to the skewers for variety.

MAKE IT AT HOME

The skewers can be cooked in a ridged grill pan on a stove top or under the broiler. The peanut sauce can be made up to 1 week ahead and stored, covered, in the refrigerator until ready to use. Bring the sauce to room temperature before serving.

Grilled Whole Chicken with Garlic-Herb Butter

Grilling a chicken whole helps it retain its moisture and flavor. Follow the simple instructions below to flatten the chicken, and grill starting with the bone side down, which will help it cook evenly. A sharp pair of kitchen shears makes the prep work easy, but a sharp knife will do—just be careful! Using a barbecue or grill with a lid will speed the cooking. If you're without a cover, be sure to situate the grill at least 6 inches from the heat source.

    1 whole chicken, about 3 to 4 pounds
    Salt and pepper
    1 recipe Garlic-Herb Butter (see
        recipe, page 60), softened

Rinse the chicken well, inside and out, discarding the giblets, and pat dry with paper towels.

Using kitchen shears or a sharp knife (use extra caution with a knife), carefully remove the backbone by cutting along both sides of it. Turn the chicken over and carefully cut out the bone running up the middle between the breasts, which will enable the chicken to lie flat. Trim off any excess fat.

Season the chicken with salt and pepper. Gently slide your fingers under the skin of the breast and the upper part of the legs to loosen it. Spread 2 to 3 tablespoons Garlic-Herb Butter under the skin. Spread another tablespoon of Garlic-Herb Butter over the outside of the chicken.

Grill the chicken over medium heat (with the lid closed if you're using a barbecue or grill with a top), starting with the bones facing down toward the fire, for 8 to 10 minutes. Baste the chicken with more

Garlic-Herb Butter and turn over (close the lid if available). Continue cooking, turning the chicken over about every 10 minutes, basting with herb butter each time you turn it—30 to 35 minutes if you use a covered grill, 50 to 60 minutes without a lid—until the chicken is cooked through. Carve or cut it into quarters and serve hot.

Serves 4

MAKE IT AT HOME

This chicken is best cooked over hot coals, but roasting the bird in an oven will also give good results—and you can cook it whole without removing the backbone and breastbone. Roasting the chicken in the oven also allows you to save the drippings and make a quick pan sauce.

Preheat the oven to 400°F. Rinse the chicken and discard the giblets. Gently slide your fingers under the skin of the breast and the upper part of the legs to loosen it. Spread 2 to 3 tablespoons of the Garlic-Herb Butter under the skin. Spread 1 tablespoon of the Garlic-Herb Butter over the outside of the chicken. Place the chicken in a roasting pan. Peel and quarter 2 medium onions and place around the chicken in the pan.

Roast the chicken, basting occasionally with additional Garlic-Herb Butter, about 1 hour, until the skin is golden and the chicken is cooked through. Drain the juices from the chicken cavity into the roasting pan. Transfer the chicken to a cutting board or serving platter and cover loosely with foil.

Set the roasting pan over medium-high heat on the stove top. Add $1/2$ cup each white wine and chicken broth, and bring to a simmer, scraping the browned bits from the bottom of the pan. Skim the fat from the sauce and discard. Transfer the sauce to a saucepan and bring to a simmer over medium heat. Mix 1 tablespoon Garlic-Herb Butter and 1 tablespoon flour in a small bowl until well combined. Stir the butter mixture into the sauce and continue to simmer, about 5 minutes more, until the sauce thickens slightly. Season to taste with salt and pepper.

Carve the chicken and serve with the sauce.

Indian-Style Curry Yogurt Chicken

Marinating chicken in yogurt makes it extremely tender and helps the flavorful spices permeate the meat. Cucumber Salad (see recipe, page 94) and rice make perfect accompaniments. A dollop of mango chutney would be a decadent touch.

  1 cup plain yogurt
  1 clove garlic, minced
  1 tablespoon peeled and minced fresh ginger
  Juice of 1 lemon
  2 tablespoons curry powder
  $1/4$ to $1/2$ teaspoon cayenne, or to taste
  1 teaspoon salt
  4 skinless, boneless chicken breast halves

Mix the yogurt, garlic, ginger, lemon juice, curry, cayenne, and salt in a large ziplock bag until well combined. Add the chicken, and turn to coat. Marinate the chicken for at least 1 hour and up to 24 hours.

Remove the chicken from the marinade (discard the marinade), and grill over medium-high heat, about 12 minutes per side, until cooked through. Serve immediately.

Serves 4

MAKE IT AT HOME

Ideal for grilling, this recipe also works well baked in an oven. Prepare the marinade and marinate the chicken as directed. Preheat the oven to 400°F. Place the chicken and marinade in a baking dish, and bake, about 20 minutes, until the chicken is cooked through. Serve immediately.

Mojo Chicken

The citrus marinade is simple to make and adds lots of fresh, bright flavor to the meat. Serve this chicken hot off the grill, or add it to a crisp green salad with Citrus Salad Dressing (see recipe, page 44) and chunks of sweet, ripe mango.

4 boneless, skinless chicken breast halves
1 large clove garlic, minced
2 teaspoons salt
2/3 cup orange juice or juice of 2 oranges
Juice of 2 lemons
Juice of 2 limes
1 tablespoon honey
1/2 teaspoon pepper
1 teaspoon ground cumin
2 tablespoons chopped fresh oregano or
  2 teaspoons crumbled dried oregano
1/3 cup olive oil

MAKE IT AT HOME

Prepare as directed and cook in a ridged grill pan or heavy skillet over medium-high heat on the stove top. Serve immediately.

Place the chicken in a ziplock bag placed flat on a table or other firm, flat surface, and pound to 1-inch thickness, using the side of an unopened can or other smooth, heavy object as a mallet.

Mash the garlic with the salt, using the back of a fork, then mix with all the remaining ingredients (except the chicken) until well combined. Add the marinade to the bag with the chicken, seal, place in a cooler, and let marinate at least 30 minutes and up to 8 hours.

Grill the chicken over medium heat, basting often with the marinade, about 5 minutes per side, until cooked through. Serve immediately, or cool, slice, and add to a mixed green salad.

Serves 4

Soy-Glazed Chicken Breasts

The sweet-salty glaze makes these chicken breasts irresistible. Use chicken wings instead and this dish is a great snack or appetizer. For a complete meal, serve with plain rice and Thai Cabbage Salad (see recipe, page 99).

4 half chicken breasts, with skin and bones
Honey-Soy Marinade (see recipe, page 45)

Place the chicken breasts with the marinade in a large ziplock bag. Marinate for at least 1 hour and up to 24 hours. Remove the chicken from the marinade, reserving the liquid, and place on a grill over medium-high heat. Cook the chicken, basting regularly with the extra marinade, about 10 minutes per side, until cooked through.

While the chicken is cooking, bring the extra marinade to a boil in a small saucepan over medium heat. Cook, stirring, at least 5 minutes, until the sauce thickens. Serve the chicken hot with the extra sauce.

Serves 4

MAKE IT AT HOME

Prepare and marinate the chicken as directed. Cook over medium-high heat in a ridged grill pan or heavy skillet on the stove top.

Spicy Orange Chicken

The combination of tangy-sweet orange, spicy red pepper, and aromatic fennel gives this dish an air of sophistication, yet it takes only a few minutes to prepare. Serve with Olive, Orange, and Couscous Salad (see recipe, page 98) and Grilled Zucchini (see recipe, page 170).

  4 boneless, skinless chicken breast halves
  Juice and grated zest of 1 orange
  1 tablespoon brown sugar
  1 clove garlic, minced
  1½ teaspoons crushed fennel seeds (crush seeds in a plastic bag, using an unopened can)
  ½ teaspoon crushed red pepper, or to taste
  1 teaspoon salt
  2 tablespoons olive oil

Place the chicken in a ziplock bag placed flat on a table or other firm, flat surface, and pound to 1-inch thickness, using the side of an unopened can or other smooth, heavy object as a mallet.

Mix the orange juice and zest, brown sugar, garlic, fennel seeds, red pepper, salt, and olive oil in a small bowl or saucepan until well combined. Add to the bag containing the chicken. Seal the bag and place in a cooler to marinate for at least 30 minutes and up to 8 hours. Remove the chicken from the marinade, reserving the liquid, and grill over medium-high heat, basting with the marinade, 5 to 7 minutes per side, until the chicken is cooked through. Discard the remaining marinade and serve immediately.

Serves 4

MAKE IT AT HOME

Prepare as directed, and cook in a ridged grill pan or heavy skillet over medium-high heat on the stove top, about 5 to 7 minutes per side, until the chicken is cooked through. Discard the remaining marinade and serve immediately.

Barbecued Peking Duck Wraps

Cucumber Salad (see recipe, page 94) and a bottle of pinot noir are all you need to make this a meal. Substitute chicken breasts for the duck, if desired.

1 whole boneless duck breast (about 1½ pounds)
¼ cup honey
¼ cup rice vinegar
¾ cup orange juice
1 tablespoon soy sauce
8 flour tortillas
⅔ cup hoisin sauce*
4 green onions, thinly sliced
2 cups shredded cabbage or lettuce

Using a sharp knife, cut several slashes through the skin and fat layer of the duck breast (do not cut into the meat below). Mix the honey, vinegar, orange juice, and soy sauce in a large ziplock bag. Add the duck to the bag, seal, and turn over several times until the duck is well coated. Place in a cooler and marinate at least 1 hour and up to 8 hours.

Grill the duck over medium-high heat, skin-side down, about 8 minutes. Turn over and cook another 8 minutes or until browned, crisp, and cooked to desired doneness (if using chicken instead of duck, be sure to cook through). Remove from the heat, cover loosely with foil, and let rest for about 5 minutes.

MAKE IT AT HOME

Prepare the marinade, and score and marinate the duck breast as directed. Preheat the oven to 400°F. Remove the duck from the marinade, reserving the marinade. Sear the breast over medium-high heat in a skillet, skin-side down, 4 to 5 minutes, until browned. Turn over and sear the other side 4 to 5 minutes, until browned. Pour the reserved marinade over the duck breast and roast, basting frequently, about 20 minutes more, until cooked through. Proceed with the recipe as directed.

Meanwhile, heat the tortillas on a grill. Slice the duck thinly across the grain (remove the skin and fat layer, if desired).

Serve the sliced duck breast with the warm tortillas, hoisin sauce, green onion, and cabbage or lettuce. Let people make their own burrito-style rolls by spreading some of the hoisin sauce down the middle of a tortilla, topping with several slices of duck breast, green onion, and cabbage or lettuce, and rolling up the tortilla.

Serves 4

* Hoisin sauce is a Chinese condiment and cooking ingredient made of ground soybeans, garlic, chiles, and spices. Find it in Asian markets or in the Asian food aisle of many supermarkets.

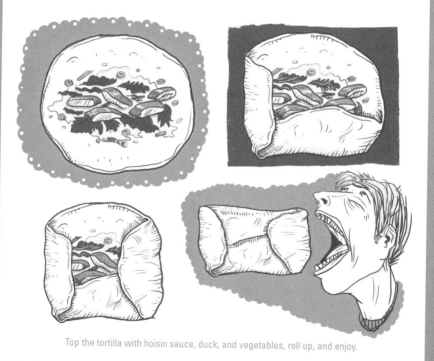

Top the tortilla with hoisin sauce, duck, and vegetables, roll up, and enjoy.

Cajun Spice–Rubbed Pork Tenderloin

Serve this spicy grilled pork with Creole Slaw (see recipe, page 93). Leftovers make great sandwiches.

   2 pork tenderloins, about 1½ pounds total
   Cajun Spice Rub (see recipe, page 49)

Rub the spice mixture over the pork tenderloins, place the meat in a large ziplock bag, and marinate in a cooler for at least 30 minutes and up to 24 hours.

   Grill the meat over medium-high heat, turning regularly, 20 to 25 minutes, until cooked through. Remove from the heat, cover loosely with foil, and let rest at least 5 minutes. Cut the pork into thin slices and serve immediately.

Serves 4

MAKE IT AT HOME

Prepare as directed, and cook in a ridged grill pan over medium-high heat on the stove top. Alternatively, preheat the oven to 400°F, sear the meat over high heat on the stove top, and then roast it about 30 minutes, until cooked through.

Maple Mustard Pork Chops

Serve these sweet-glazed pork chops with grilled sweet potatoes and a crisp green salad.

1/4 cup Dijon mustard
2 tablespoons balsamic vinegar
I teaspoon salt
1/2 teaspoon pepper
I cup maple syrup
4 boneless pork chops

MAKE IT AT HOME

Prepare as directed. Cook the chops in a ridged grill pan or heavy skillet over medium-high heat on the stove top, or broil the chops under the broiler, about 15 minutes, until cooked through.

Mix the mustard, vinegar, salt, pepper, and syrup in a large ziplock bag until well combined. Add the pork chops, seal the bag, and marinate in a cooler at least I hour and up to 24 hours.

Remove the pork chops from the marinade, and transfer the remaining marinade to a small saucepan. Bring the marinade to a boil over high heat on a camp stove, reduce the heat to medium, and simmer, stirring occasionally, for at least 5 minutes.

While the glaze is cooking, grill the pork chops over medium-high heat, basting with some of the marinade occasionally, about 7 minutes per side, until cooked through. Serve immediately with the extra marinade drizzled over the top. (Be sure the marinade has cooked for at least 5 minutes before serving.)

Serves 4

Beer-Brined Pork and Onion Skewers

Marinating pork in beer, sugar, and salt makes it exceptionally tender and flavorful.

- 1 1/2 cups water
- 1 bottle beer
- 1/2 cup packed brown sugar
- 1 tablespoon crumbled dried oregano
- 2 cloves garlic, minced
- 1/4 cup salt
- 1 teaspoon pepper
- 1 1/2 pounds pork loin or pork butt, cut into 2-inch chunks
- 2 medium onions, cut into 2-inch chunks

Mix the water, beer, sugar, oregano, garlic, salt, and pepper in a large ziplock bag until well combined. Add the pork chunks to the bag and shake to combine. Seal the bag, and marinate in a cooler for at least 4 hours and up to 48 hours.

Remove the pork from the marinade, and discard the liquid. Thread the pork chunks and onion chunks alternately onto skewers. Grill the skewers over medium-high heat, turning regularly, 15 to 20 minutes, until the pork is cooked through. Let stand 5 minutes before serving.

Serves 4

MAKE IT AT HOME

Prepare the brining liquid as directed and use it to brine a pork loin roast. Marinate the pork up to 72 hours. Bring the roast to room temperature before cooking. Preheat the oven to 450°F. Sear the roast over high heat on the stove top, then roast with onion chunks scattered around the meat, turning occasionally, 45 minutes to 1 hour, until the pork is cooked through.

Jambalaya

I like to make this Louisiana classic with spicy andouille sausage, shrimp, and chicken broth. Substituting vegetarian sausage and vegetable broth and leaving out the shrimp transform it into a satisfying meat-free option. Although at first glance this may seem like a lot of ingredients, most are staples you probably already have in your camp kitchen.

- 2 tablespoons olive oil
- 1 large onion, diced
- 2 cloves garlic, minced
- 2 green bell peppers, seeded and diced
- 1 pound andouille or other spicy sausage, or vegetarian sausage, sliced
- 1 tablespoon chili powder
- 2 teaspoons dried thyme
- 1/2 to 1 teaspoon cayenne
- 1 teaspoon salt
- 1 14-ounce can diced tomatoes, drained
- 2 14-ounce cans chicken or vegetable broth
- 1 1/2 cups uncooked white rice
- 1 pound shrimp, peeled (optional)

Heat the oil in a large pot over medium-high heat on a camp stove. Add the onion, garlic, and bell pepper, and cook, stirring, about 5 minutes, until the onion is soft and translucent. Add the sausage, chili powder, thyme, cayenne, and salt. Stir to combine, and cook for about 1 minute. Add the tomatoes, broth, and rice. Bring the mixture to a simmer, reduce the heat to low, cover, and cook, stirring occasionally, about 30 minutes, until the rice is tender. Add the shrimp, if using, and cook, stirring, about 3 minutes more, until cooked through. Serve hot.

Serves 4 to 6

* Recipe is vegetarian if made with vegetable sausage and vegetable broth and shrimp is left out.

Grilled Steak with Five-Spice Rub

Chinese five-spice powder* (a combination of cinnamon, anise, cloves, ginger, and fennel) lends an exotic flavor to this grilled steak. Give it a tropical twist by serving it with a generous spoonful of Tropical Fruit Salsa (see recipe, page 104). If using one large steak, such as flank or skirt steak, be sure to let the steak rest for 5 minutes before slicing it so that the meat reabsorbs its juices.

    1 tablespoon brown sugar
    1 tablespoon Chinese five-spice powder
    1 tablespoon peeled and minced fresh ginger
    1 teaspoon salt
    1 flank or skirt steak (about 1 1/2 pounds) or 4 T-bone or
    New York steaks

Mix the brown sugar, five-spice powder, ginger, and salt in a small bowl until well combined. Rub the spice mixture over both sides of the steak. Grill the steak over medium-high heat, 5 to 6 minutes per side, until cooked to the desired doneness.

MAKE IT AT HOME

Prepare as directed. Cook the steak in a ridged grill pan or heavy skillet over medium-high heat on the stove top, or broil, 6 to 8 minutes per side, until cooked to the desired doneness. Continue with the preparation as directed.

If using flank or skirt steak, remove the steak from the grill, cover loosely with foil, and let rest about 5 minutes. Slice the steak across the grain into 1/8-inch-thick slices. Serve immediately.

Serves 4

* Chinese five-spice powder is available in the spice section of most supermarkets.

Grilled Flank Steak with Olive Relish

Olive Oil Roasted Potatoes (see recipe, page 177) and a salad of mixed greens dressed with Basic Vinaigrette Dressing (see recipe, page 43) make this a satisfying meal.

> 1 cup dry red wine
> 1/2 cup soy sauce
> 1/4 cup olive oil
> 1 tablespoon Dijon mustard
> 1 1/2 pounds flank steak
> Olive Relish (see recipe, page 59)

Mix the wine, soy sauce, olive oil, and mustard in a large ziplock bag until well combined. Add the steak to the bag, seal, and shake to coat the meat completely. Place in a cooler and marinate for at least 1 hour and up to 24 hours.

Grill the steak over medium–high heat, 5 to 6 minutes per side, until cooked to the desired doneness.

MAKE IT AT HOME

Prepare as directed. Cook the steak in a ridged grill pan or heavy skillet over medium-high heat on the stove top, or broil, 6 to 8 minutes per side, until cooked to the desired doneness. Serve with scalloped potatoes.

Remove the steak from the grill and let it rest, loosely covered with foil, about 5 minutes. Slice the steak across the grain into 1/8-inch-thick slices and serve topped with Olive Relish.

Serves 4

Grilled Flank Steak with Yogurt Mint Sauce

Though this sauce is simple to make at camp, it can be made at home to bring along, as it will keep for several days. For a complete meal, serve this dish with a lettuce and tomato salad topped with crumbled feta cheese and Honey-Lemon Vinaigrette (see recipe, page 44), along with pita rounds warmed on the grill for scooping up the extra sauce.

 Juice of 2 lemons
 2 tablespoons olive oil
 1/2 teaspoon salt
 1/2 teaspoon pepper
 1 1/2 pounds flank steak
 Yogurt Mint Sauce (see recipe, page 57)

Mix the lemon juice, olive oil, salt, and pepper in a large ziplock bag until well combined. Add the steak to the bag, seal, and shake to make sure the steak is fully coated with marinade. Place in a cooler and marinate at least 1 hour and up to 24 hours.

Grill the steak over medium-high heat, 6 to 8 minutes per side, until cooked to the desired doneness. Remove the steak to a cutting board, cover loosely with foil, and let rest for 5 minutes before serving.

Cut the steak into thin slices diagonally across the grain. Serve the sliced steak with a dollop of Yogurt Mint Sauce.

Serves 4

MAKE IT AT HOME

Prepare as directed. Cook the steak over medium heat in a ridged grill pan or heavy skillet on the stove top, or broil, 6 to 8 minutes per side, until cooked to the desired doneness.

Grilled Steak Tacos

A simple marinade flavors this steak. Set out all the fixings, and let people assemble their own tacos. Serve with Black Bean Salad (see recipe, page 92) or purchased refried beans.

    1½ pounds flank or skirt steak
    Red Wine Marinade (see recipe, page 46), made with lime juice
    Corn tortillas
    Shredded lettuce
    Lime wedges
    Chopped Tomato Salsa (see recipe, page 104)
      or Fire-Roasted Salsa (see recipe, page 105)
    Sliced radishes (optional)
    Simply Perfect Guacamole (optional, see
      recipe, page 103)

MAKE IT AT HOME

Marinate the steak as directed. Cook in a ridged grill pan or heavy skillet on the stove top, or broil, 6 to 8 minutes per side, until cooked to desired doneness. Continue with the preparation as directed.

Place the steak in a large ziplock bag. Pour the marinade into the bag with the steak. Seal the bag, place in a cooler, and marinate at least 1 hour and up to 24 hours.

Grill the steak over high heat, 5 to 7 minutes per side, until cooked to the desired doneness. Remove the steak to a cutting board, cover loosely with foil, and let rest for 5 minutes. Meanwhile, grill the tortillas over the fire until warm. Slice the steak into ¼-inch-thick strips and serve with the warm tortillas, lettuce, lime wedges, salsa, radishes, and guacamole (if using).

Serves 4

Hoisin-Glazed Beef Kebabs

For easy handling, thread 2 skewers through the beef cubes (the skewers should be parallel to each other, about 1/4 inch apart). This keeps the meat from spinning when you turn them over. Rice and Cucumber Salad (see recipe, page 94) round out the meal perfectly.

    4 green onions, thinly sliced
    1 recipe Hoisin Glaze (see recipe, page 54)
    1 1/2 pounds beef top sirloin, cut into 1 1/2-inch cubes

Mix the green onion and the Hoisin Glaze in a large bowl, pot, or ziplock bag until well combined. Add the beef and marinate in a cooler about 15 minutes (or up to 24 hours, if desired). Remove the beef from the marinade, and transfer the remaining liquid to a saucepan. Thread the beef onto skewers, and grill over medium-high heat, turning and basting with some of the reserved marinade, 10 to 12 minutes, until cooked through.

> **MAKE IT AT HOME**
>
> Prepare as directed. Cook the meat in a ridged grill pan over medium-high heat on the stove top, or broil, 6 to 8 minutes per side, until cooked to the desired doneness. Continue with the preparation as directed.

While the meat is cooking, bring the reserved marinade to a boil over high heat. Reduce the heat to medium and simmer, stirring frequently, until the sauce thickens. The sauce should cook for at least 5 minutes before serving.

When the beef is cooked to the desired doneness, serve immediately with some of the extra sauce drizzled over the top.

Serves 4

Variations:

- Substitute 1 1/2 pounds cubed boneless, skinless chicken breast for the beef.
- If you don't want to bother with skewers, use 1 1/2 pounds skirt or flank steak in place of the cubed beef. Grill over medium-high heat, 6 to 8 minutes per side, until cooked to the desired doneness. Cut into slices.
- Instead of beef, use 1/2-inch-thick lamb or pork chops. Grill over medium-high heat, 4 to 6 minutes per side, until cooked to the desired doneness.

Mustard and Rosemary Lamb Chops

Flavorful lamb chops are worth the splurge. Ideally, lamb should be served rare, never well done. I like to use thinner chops and serve 2 per person, but you may prefer thicker cuts. If so, simply adjust your cooking time according to the thickness of your meat (see "Is It Done Yet?," page 30).

2/3 cup olive oil
1/3 cup Dijon mustard
2 cloves garlic, minced
I teaspoon salt
1/2 teaspoon pepper
2 tablespoons chopped fresh rosemary
8 lamb chops, 3/4 inch to I inch thick (about 2 pounds total)

Mix the olive oil, mustard, garlic, salt, pepper, and rosemary in a large bowl or ziplock bag until well combined. Add the lamb chops and marinate about 15 minutes (or up to 24 hours, if desired). Grill the chops over high heat, basting often, 4 to 6 minutes per side, until cooked to the desired doneness. Serve immediately.

Serves 4

MAKE IT AT HOME

Prepare the marinade and marinate the meat as directed. Preheat the broiler. Just before cooking, dredge the chops in bread crumbs (about 1 cup total). Cook the chops under the broiler, 4 to 6 minutes per side, until cooked to the desired doneness.

Grilled Eggplant Parmesan

Salting eggplant before cooking it extracts excess moisture, which allows it to absorb the flavors of the other ingredients. You'll need a good pair of tongs and a spatula to maneuver these gooey eggplant, tomato, and cheese "sandwiches" on the grill. I like to serve them topped with Easy Tomato Sauce (see recipe, page 58, or use a purchased pasta sauce).

2 medium eggplants, cut lengthwise into $1/2$-inch-thick slices
1 tablespoon salt
4 medium tomatoes, chopped
$1/2$ cup chopped fresh basil
2 cloves garlic, minced
$1/2$ teaspoon salt
$1/2$ teaspoon pepper
Olive oil spray or non-stick cooking spray
6 ounces Monterey Jack or mozzarella cheese, thinly sliced
$1/4$ cup grated Parmesan cheese

Sprinkle the eggplant slices with 1 tablespoon salt, place in a colander or on several layers of paper towels, and set aside for about 30 minutes.

Mix the tomato, basil, garlic, $1/2$ teaspoon salt, and pepper in a small bowl or saucepan until well combined.

Pat the eggplant slices dry with paper towels and spray on both sides with olive oil spray. Grill the eggplant slices over medium heat on one side, 4 to 6 minutes, until grill marks appear and the

MAKE IT AT HOME

Preheat the oven to 400°F. Salt the eggplant and prepare the tomato mixture as directed. Butter or oil a 10-inch-square baking dish. Pat the eggplant slices dry with paper towels, and place several in a single layer covering the bottom of the baking dish. Top with some of the tomato mixture and some of the Jack or mozzarella cheese. Top with another layer of eggplant slices, then tomato mixture, then cheese. Continue until all the eggplant slices, tomato mixture, and cheese have been used, ending with a layer of eggplant slices. Sprinkle the Parmesan cheese over the top. Bake, 30 to 40 minutes, until the eggplant is soft. Serve hot, topped with hot tomato sauce, if desired.

eggplant begins to soften. Turn the eggplant slices over and top half the slices with the tomato mixture and the Jack or mozzarella cheese, dividing evenly among them. When the untopped slices brown and soften on the second side, place them on top of the slices with the tomato and cheese. Sprinkle Parmesan over the top slices and continue grilling, about 2 minutes more, until the cheese melts. Serve immediately, topped with hot tomato sauce if desired.

Serves 4

Grilled Flatbread Pizzas

Who doesn't like a hot, bubbly pizza? Using lavash* makes this recipe easily doable just about anywhere. Be sure to cook these over medium, not hot, coals, or the thin bread will burn to a crisp in seconds.

    2 cloves garlic, minced
    1 cup tomato sauce (canned is fine)
    2 24- by 9-inch soft lavash, halved crosswise, or 4 6-inch pitas, split
    Olive oil spray or nonstick cooking spray
    1½ cups (8 to 10 ounces) fresh mozzarella, thinly sliced, or
        regular mozzarella, shredded
    2 tablespoons chopped fresh basil or 2 teaspoons dried basil

Stir the garlic into the tomato sauce. Spray the flatbread on one side with olive oil spray. Spread a thin layer of tomato sauce over the unoiled side, then a layer of the cheese, then basil. Place on the grill and cook until browned on the bottom and the cheese is melted, about 5 minutes. Cut into pieces and serve immediately.

Serves 4

Variations:

- **Greek Pizza** Top the flatbreads with the tomato sauce, 8 ounces crumbled feta cheese, 1 clove minced garlic, ½ cup chopped kalamata olives, and 2 tablespoons chopped fresh oregano.
- **Caramelized Onion, Gruyère, and Bacon Pizza** Top the flatbreads with caramelized onion (3 medium onions, thinly sliced and cooked in a skillet over medium heat on the camp stove in 3 tablespoons olive oil until very soft and golden); 8 ounces shredded Gruyère cheese; 3 strips bacon, cooked and crumbled; and 2 tablespoons chopped fresh thyme.

> ## MAKE IT AT HOME
>
> Preheat the oven to 450°F. Top the flatbread with your desired toppings, and bake directly on the oven rack, about 5 minutes, until the bread is crisp and golden and the cheese is melted.

* Lavash is a Middle Eastern flatbread, available in specialty food stores or in the ethnic food aisle or bread aisle of many supermarkets.

Tofu Steaks with Red Wine–Mushroom Sauce

This classic reduction sauce works just as well with grilled tofu as it does with steak.

- 3 tablespoons olive oil
- 2 medium shallots or 1 small onion, finely chopped
- 4 cups chopped mushrooms (use a mixture of shiitakes, creminis, portobellos, etc.)
- 2 1/4 cups red wine
- 1 1/2 tablespoons chopped fresh thyme or 1 1/2 teaspoons dried thyme
- 1/2 teaspoon salt
- 1/2 teaspoon pepper
- Olive oil spray or nonstick cooking spray
- 24 ounces (1 1/2 16-ounce packages) water-packed super-firm or firm tofu, drained

Heat the olive oil in a large skillet over medium-high heat on a camp stove. Add the shallot or onion and sauté 1 minute. Add the mushrooms and continue cooking, stirring occasionally, 6 to 8 minutes, until the mushrooms are soft and their liquid has evaporated. Add the wine, thyme, salt, and pepper, and bring to a boil. Cook, about 15 minutes, until reduced by half.

While the sauce is cooking, cut the tofu lengthwise into 3/4-inch-thick slices and lightly coat each slice with olive oil spray. Grill the tofu over high heat, 3 to 4 minutes on each side, until browned. Serve the tofu topped with the mushrooms and sauce.

Serves 4

Variation:

For added richness, sprinkle each sauce-topped piece of tofu with 1 tablespoon crumbled blue cheese or shaved Parmesan.

Vietnamese Lettuce Wraps with Spicy Grilled Tofu

In this spicy vegetarian entrée, lettuce leaves serve as wrappers for a Southeast Asian–style burrito.

Juice of 2 limes

$^1/_4$ cup honey

$^1/_4$ cup soy sauce

I teaspoon Asian chile paste or chile paste with garlic

I clove garlic, minced (omit if using chile paste with garlic)

24 ounces (1$^1/_2$ 16-ounce packages) water-packed firm tofu, drained and sliced into $^1/_2$-inch pieces

I head iceberg lettuce leaves

$^1/_2$ cup cilantro leaves

$^1/_2$ cup mint leaves

$^1/_2$ cup basil leaves

$^1/_4$ cup dry-roasted peanuts, crushed slightly

2 jalapeño chiles, thinly sliced

Mix the lime juice, honey, soy sauce, chile paste, and garlic in a large ziplock bag until well combined. Add the tofu, and turn to coat. Marinate the tofu in a cooler for at least I hour.

Remove the tofu from the bag and reserve the marinade. Grill the tofu over medium-high heat, about 5 minutes per side, until browned.

Serve the tofu with the reserved marinade, lettuce leaves, and other garnishes. To eat, place a piece of tofu on a lettuce leaf, garnish with the cilantro, mint, basil,

MAKE IT AT HOME

Before cooking, place the tofu slices on a double layer of paper towels. Top with 2 more layers of paper towels, then top with a baking dish or heavy plate. Let sit about 5 minutes to squeeze out excess water. Marinate the drained tofu in a mixture of $^1/_4$ cup soy sauce, juice of 1 lime, and 1 tablespoon vegetable oil for about 5 minutes. Cook the tofu in a ridged grill pan over medium-high heat on the stove top. Serve as directed.

peanuts, and chiles as desired. Drizzle a bit of sauce over the top, and wrap the lettuce around the toppings.

Serves 4

White Bean Stew

This hearty vegetarian stew is a simple way to satisfy big appetites.

- 1/4 cup olive oil
- 4 cloves garlic, minced
- 1 large red onion, chopped
- 4 large tomatoes, chopped
- 2 14-ounce cans white beans (such as cannellini, great northern, or navy), drained and rinsed
- 1 teaspoon salt
- 1 teaspoon pepper
- 2 tablespoons chopped fresh rosemary
- 1/2 cup grated Parmesan cheese

Heat the oil in a 2-quart pot over medium-high heat on a camp stove. Add the garlic and onion and cook, stirring, until the onion is soft and translucent, about 5 minutes. Add the tomato, beans, salt, pepper, and rosemary. Cook until heated through, 5 to 10 minutes more. Sprinkle the cheese over to serve.

Serves 4

MAKE IT AT HOME

Preheat the oven to 475°F. Prepare and cook as directed on the stove top, using a pot that can be placed in the oven. Mix the cheese with 1/2 cup bread crumbs and sprinkle over the top. Place the pot, uncovered, in the oven and bake, about 10 minutes, until the top is golden brown. Serve hot.

White Beans with Lemon and Mint

This dish, with the refreshing flavor combination of lemon and mint, tastes like spring any time of year.

2 14-ounce cans white beans (cannellini, great northern, or navy), drained and rinsed

4 cups water

1 teaspoon salt plus seasoning, to taste

2 tablespoons olive oil

Juice and finely grated zest of 1 lemon

1/2 cup packed chopped fresh mint leaves

1/2 teaspoon pepper

2 ounces Parmesan cheese, grated (optional)

Place the beans, water, and salt in a medium pot. Bring to a boil over high heat on a camp stove. Lower the heat to medium and simmer about 10 minutes. Drain the beans and stir in the olive oil, lemon juice and zest, mint, and pepper. Stir until well mixed, taste for seasoning, and add more salt if needed. Serve warm, topped with the grated Parmesan cheese, if desired.

Serves 4

Orzo with Wild Mushrooms and Peas

Orzo is tiny, rice-shaped pasta. It's great for camping since you can cook it in broth, like a risotto, without having to drain it. Because all the ingredients will last a long time, this satisfying vegetarian entrée or side dish is a perfect meal for late in a longer trip.

  2 ounces dried porcini mushrooms
  2 cups hot (not boiling) water
  2 tablespoons olive oil or butter
  1 large shallot or 1 small yellow onion, diced
  1 cup orzo
  1 teaspoon salt
  $1/2$ teaspoon pepper
  1 cup fresh or frozen (unthawed is fine) peas
  4 ounces grated Parmesan cheese, plus more for serving, if desired

Place the dried mushrooms in a small bowl and pour the hot water over them. Set aside to rehydrate for 20 to 30 minutes. Remove the mushrooms from the liquid, and reserve the liquid. Chop the mushrooms into rough pieces.

Heat the oil or butter in a large skillet over medium-high heat on a camp stove. Add the shallot or onion and cook, stirring frequently, about 5 minutes, until translucent. Add the mushrooms and orzo and cook, stirring, about 1 minute. Add the salt and pepper. Pour in the reserved liquid from the mushrooms, being careful to leave behind any sandy sediment. Bring to a boil, reduce the heat to medium-low, cover, and simmer, about 10 minutes, until the orzo is tender and most of the liquid has been absorbed. Add the peas and continue to cook, stirring, until the peas are hot, 2 to 3 minutes. Remove from the heat, stir in the grated Parmesan, and serve immediately, with more cheese grated over the top, if desired.

Serves 4

Grilled Tofu with Coconut Curry Sauce

This spicy sauce is so addictive you may be tempted to spoon up and eat any that's left over. Instead, save it to serve over grilled cauliflower or as a dipping sauce for grilled chicken or shrimp skewers.

24 ounces (1½ 16-ounce packages) water-packed super-firm or firm tofu, drained

Olive oil spray or nonstick cooking spray

Coconut Curry Sauce (see recipe, page 52)

4 green onions, thinly sliced

Cut the tofu lengthwise into 3/4-inch-thick slices and lightly coat each slice with olive oil spray. Grill the tofu over high heat, about 4 minutes per side, until browned. Serve the tofu topped with curry sauce and green onion slices.

Serves 4

MAKE IT AT HOME

Before cooking, place the tofu slices on a double layer of paper towels. Top with 2 more layers of paper towels, then top with a baking dish or heavy plate. Let sit about 5 minutes to squeeze out excess water. Marinate the drained tofu in a mixture of ¼ cup soy sauce, 1 teaspoon sesame oil, and 1 tablespoon vegetable oil for about 5 minutes. Cook the tofu as directed, using a ridged grill pan or heavy skillet on the stove top. Serve topped with Coconut Curry Sauce.

Goat Cheese Quesadillas with Tomato and Corn Salsa

Tangy goat cheese pairs well with spicy salsa for a quick and delicious appetizer or vegetarian entrée. Serve these with extra salsa and Simply Perfect Guacamole (see recipe, page 103).

Olive oil spray or nonstick cooking spray
8 10-inch flour tortillas
12 ounces soft fresh goat cheese, crumbled (about 1½ cups)
Tomato and Corn Salsa (see recipe, page 104)

GRILL METHOD:

Spray one side of a tortilla with oil and place it, oiled side down, on the grill over medium-high heat. Top with one-quarter (about 3 ounces) of the cheese and one-quarter of the salsa. Spray one side of a second tortilla with oil, and place it on top of the first, oiled side up. Cook, about 3 minutes, until the bottom tortilla is golden brown. Turn the quesadilla over and continue cooking, about 3 minutes more, until the bottom is golden brown and the cheese is melted. Remove from the grill and cut into wedges. Repeat with the remaining tortillas, cheese, and salsa. Serve immediately.

MAKE IT AT HOME

Make it a meal by adding broiled shrimp. Preheat the broiler. Spread 1 pound of peeled shrimp in a single layer on a baking sheet, spray with olive oil, and season with salt and pepper. Broil, about 2 minutes, until the shrimp is cooked through. Split each shrimp in half lengthwise. Continue with preparation per the camp-stove method, substituting Fire-Roasted Salsa (see recipe, page 105). Add ¼ cup of the shrimp to each quesadilla along with the cheese and salsa.

CAMP-STOVE METHOD:

Spray a large skillet with oil and warm over medium-high heat on the stove. Place 1 tortilla in the hot skillet, and top with one-quarter (about 3 ounces) of the cheese and one-quarter of the salsa. Top with a second tortilla. Cook, about 3 minutes, until the bottom tortilla is golden brown. Turn the quesadilla over and continue cooking, about 3 minutes more, until the bottom is golden brown and the cheese is melted. Remove from the skillet and cut into wedges. Repeat with the remaining tortillas, cheese, and salsa. Serve immediately.

Serves 8 to 10 as an appetizer, 4 to 6 as an entrée

Variation:

Substitute Tropical Fruit Salsa (see recipe, page 104) or Fire-Roasted Salsa (see recipe, page 105) for the Tomato and Corn Salsa.

ON THE SIDE: COOKED VEGETABLES, GRAINS, AND OTHER SIDES

For me, vegetables and grains are the true heart of a healthy meal. Mix and match these vegetables, grains, and other side dishes with the entrées in the previous chapter for well-rounded, hearty, and satisfying dinners.

Garlic and Herb Mushrooms

Sautéed mushrooms without the mess! I like to serve these in their foil packets so that I can sop up the garlicky, buttery sauce with toasted bread. You may prefer to scoop them out with a slotted spoon, leaving behind the juice, or toss the whole thing with cooked pasta and garnish with grated parmesan for a satisfying vegetarian entrée.

   Olive oil spray or nonstick cooking spray
   1½ pounds button or cremini mushrooms, quartered
   Garlic-Herb Butter (see recipe, page 60)

Prepare 4 squares of foil by spraying with olive oil spray. Place one-quarter (about 6 ounces) of the mushrooms on each square of foil. Top each mushroom pile with one-quarter of the butter mixture, dolloping it around so that it is fairly well distributed. Wrap the foil securely around the mushrooms, leaving room for heat and steam to circulate inside. Grill over high heat, 25 to 30 minutes.

Serves 4

MAKE IT AT HOME

These tidy mushroom packets can also be made in an oven. Preheat the oven to 425°F. Prepare the packets as directed, and cook, 20 to 30 minutes, until the mushrooms are soft.

Ginger-Steamed Snow Peas

Steaming vegetables in foil packets is quick, easy, and healthy. Serve these crisp-tender peas alongside Grilled Prawns with Hoisin Glaze (see recipe, page 125).

    1 pound snow peas, trimmed
    2 teaspoons peeled and minced fresh ginger
    Salt to taste
    1/2 cup chicken broth or water

Lay out 4 squares of aluminum foil and divide the snow peas evenly among them. Sprinkle the ginger over the peas, distributing evenly among the packets. Sprinkle with salt. Fold up the sides of each packet, and pour in one-quarter of the chicken broth or water. Double-fold the tops and sides of the packets, leaving room for steam to circulate around the vegetables. Grill the packets over high heat, 8 to 10 minutes, until the peas are crisp-tender. Serve immediately.

Serves 4

* Recipe is vegetarian if made with water instead of chicken broth.

MAKE IT AT HOME

Bring the broth or water to a boil in a saucepan or skillet. Add the minced ginger and salt. Place the snow peas in a steamer basket, and cover. Reduce the heat to a fast simmer, and place the steamer basket over the simmering water. Steam, 6 to 8 minutes, until the peas are crisp-tender. Serve immediately.

Grilled Asparagus

This is an ingenious way to enjoy asparagus cooked over the fire.

1¹/₂ pounds asparagus spears, trimmed
Olive oil spray or nonstick cooking spray
Salt and pepper

Lay 5 or 6 asparagus spears next to each other. Pierce through all of them crosswise with 2 skewers, one near their tops and one near their bases, to form a sort of asparagus raft. Spray each raft with olive oil. Grill over hot coals, turning occasionally, about 15 minutes, until the spears are tender. Sprinkle the spears with salt and pepper before serving.

Serves 4

MAKE IT AT HOME

Preheat the oven to 400°F. Place the asparagus spears in a baking dish and spray with olive oil spray. Sprinkle with salt and pepper. Roast, 10 to 20 minutes, depending on the thickness of the stalks, until the spears are tender.

This technique works just as well for crookneck squash and many other vegetables.

> 4 medium zucchini
> Olive oil or nonstick cooking spray
> Salt and pepper

Slice the zucchini in half lengthwise. Spray with olive oil or cooking spray, and season with salt and pepper. Grill over medium–high heat, turning once, 10 to 15 minutes, depending on the size of your zucchini, until the zucchini is tender and beginning to brown. Serve immediately.

Serves 4

MAKE IT AT HOME

Preheat the oven to 400°F. Prepare the zucchini as directed and place, cut-side down, on a baking sheet. Roast, turning over halfway through cooking 10 to 20 minutes depending on the size of zucchini, until the zucchini is tender and beginning to brown. Serve immediately.

Grilled Cauliflower with Coconut Curry Sauce

Choose a head of cauliflower with densely packed flowers so that it will hold together well during grilling.

    1 small head cauliflower, stemmed, leaves removed,
      and quartered
    Olive oil spray or nonstick cooking spray
    1/2 teaspoon salt
    1/2 teaspoon pepper
    Coconut Curry Sauce (see recipe, page 52)

Spray the cauliflower quarters all over with olive oil, and sprinkle with the salt and pepper. Grill over medium-high heat, turning occasionally, 4 to 5 minutes per side, until soft and beginning to brown. Chop the cooked cauliflower into large chunks and serve topped with Coconut Curry Sauce.

Serves 4

Variations:
- Serve with Spicy Peanut Sauce (see recipe, page 56) instead of Coconut Curry Sauce.
- Top the grilled cauliflower with crumbled blue cheese or goat cheese, and drizzle with Balsamic Syrup (see recipe, page 51) instead of Coconut Curry Sauce.

MAKE IT AT HOME

Preheat the oven to 400°F. Coarsely chop the cauliflower, and place in a baking dish. Spray the cauliflower all over with olive oil spray, and sprinkle with the salt and pepper. Roast, stirring once or twice, about 25 minutes, until the cauliflower is tender and browned in spots. Serve topped with sauce.

Grilled Radicchio with Balsamic Syrup

Grilling radicchio gives it a smoky flavor, and the Balsamic Syrup balances its bitterness. This simple dish is sure to impress those with sophisticated palates.

4 small heads of radicchio, quartered
Olive oil spray or nonstick cooking spray
Salt and pepper
Balsamic Syrup (see recipe, page 51)
3 ounces Parmesan, shaved (optional)

Spray the radicchio quarters with olive oil, and season with salt and pepper to taste. Place the radicchio on a grill over medium-high heat. Cook, turning occasionally, about 5 minutes, until it begins to brown and soften. Serve the radicchio hot with the syrup drizzled over it, topped with shaved Parmesan, if desired.

Serves 4

MAKE IT AT HOME

Prepare as directed, cooking the radicchio in a ridged grill pan on the stove top, or roasting it in a 400°F oven, about 10 minutes, until it begins to soften and brown.

Roasted Beets with Citrus Dressing

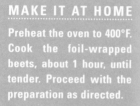

Though roasting beets takes some time, this dish is well worth the wait. Try it with Mustard and Rosemary Lamb Chops (see recipe, page 153).

    4 to 6 medium beets, trimmed
    Olive oil spray
    Citrus Salad Dressing (see recipe, page 44)
    3 ounces crumbled goat cheese or feta
      cheese (optional)

MAKE IT AT HOME

Preheat the oven to 400°F. Cook the foil-wrapped beets, about 1 hour, until tender. Proceed with the preparation as directed.

Spray the beets all over with oil, and wrap tightly in foil in 2 or 3 packets, as needed. Place the packets on a grill over medium-high heat. Cook, turning occasionally, about 1 hour, until the beets are tender.

Remove the beets from the grill, unwrap, and, when cool enough to handle, slip off the skins. Slice the beets into wedges and toss with the dressing. Serve topped with the crumbled cheese, if desired.

Serves 4

White Beans with Chanterelle Mushrooms

Roasting chanterelles in foil brings out their fruity quality.

- 2 14-ounce cans cannellini beans or other white beans, drained and rinsed
- 3/4 pound chanterelles, roughly chopped
- 2 medium shallots or 1 small red onion, chopped
- 1/4 cup olive oil
- 1 1/2 tablespoons chopped fresh thyme
- 1 teaspoon salt
- Olive oil spray or non stick cooking spray

MAKE IT AT HOME

Dry-sauté the chanterelles in a heavy pot over medium heat, stirring, about 5 minutes, until they give up their liquid and reabsorb it. Add the olive oil and shallots or onion, and cook, stirring, about 3 minutes more, until the mushrooms begin to soften. Reduce the heat to medium-low, and add the remaining ingredients and about 1/4 cup dry white wine. Cook, stirring occasionally, 15 to 20 minutes, until the mushrooms and beans are tender.

Mix the beans, mushrooms, shallot or onion, olive oil, thyme, and salt in a medium bowl or pot until well combined. Spray 4 large squares of aluminum foil with olive oil spray. Place one-quarter of the bean mixture on each square, fold up the sides, and seal the packet, leaving room for heat and steam to circulate inside. Grill over high heat, about 20 minutes, until the mushrooms are soft. Serve immediately.

Serves 4

Maple-Glazed Yams

Yams are said to be among the most nutritious of vegetables—and they're a nice change of pace from regular potatoes. Serve this sweet and savory dish alongside spicy Cajun Spice–Rubbed Pork Tenderloin (see recipe, page 144).

Olive oil spray or nonstick cooking spray
3 to 4 medium yams, peeled and diced
$1/3$ cup maple syrup
Salt
2 tablespoons butter, cut into pieces

Spray 4 squares of aluminum foil with oil and place one-quarter of the diced yam in the center of each. Drizzle the maple syrup over the yams, dividing evenly among the 4 packets. Top each packet with one-quarter of the butter. Season with salt to taste. Seal the packets, leaving room for heat and steam to circulate inside. Grill the packets over high heat, 30 to 35 minutes, until the yams are soft. Serve immediately.

Serves 4

MAKE IT AT HOME

Bake this side dish in a large baking dish in the oven, add a crunchy pecan topping, and serve with roast turkey or chicken.

Preheat the oven to 400°F. Grease a large baking dish. Blanch the yams in a large pot of boiling water for about 3 minutes, then drain. Spread the yams in the bottom of the baking dish, season with salt to taste, and drizzle the syrup over the top. Dot with the butter, cover, and bake, about 30 minutes, until the yams are tender.

Using your fingers, mix $1/4$ cup flour, $1/4$ cup brown sugar, $1/2$ teaspoon cayenne (optional), and 2 tablespoons butter until the mixture resembles coarse meal. Add $1/3$ cup chopped pecans. Sprinkle the mixture over the yams and bake, another 15 to 20 minutes, until the top is browned and crunchy. Serve hot.

Foil-Baked Yams with Spicy Chili Butter

Spicy cinnamon, chili powder, and cayenne perk up these sweet potatoes. Serve these with Mojo Chicken (see recipe, page 139) or any grilled meat.

>   Olive oil spray or nonstick cooking spray
>   3 cups yams, peeled and diced
>   Spicy Chili Butter (see recipe, page 61)

Lay out 4 squares of aluminum foil, spray with oil, and place one-quarter of the diced yams in the center of each. Top each pile of yams with about one-quarter of the butter-spice mixture, dolloping it about so that it is fairly evenly distributed. Seal the packets, leaving room for heat and steam to circulate inside. Grill the packets over high heat, 30 to 35 minutes, until the diced yam is soft. Serve immediately.

Serves 4

MAKE IT AT HOME

Preheat the oven to 375°F. Prepare as directed, placing the diced yams in an oiled baking dish. Top with Spicy Chili Butter and bake, uncovered, 35 to 40 minutes, until the diced yams are tender.

Olive Oil Roasted Potatoes

These tasty potatoes are a perfect accompaniment to grilled meat or fish.

- 4 medium shallots, peeled and thinly sliced
- 1 pound small red new potatoes, halved or quartered if large
- $^1/_4$ cup olive oil
- 1 tablespoon chopped fresh rosemary or thyme
- 1 teaspoon salt
- 1 teaspoon pepper

Mix the shallot slices and potatoes in a large bowl or pot until well combined. Toss with the olive oil, rosemary or thyme, salt, and pepper until the vegetables are well coated.

Lay out 4 squares of aluminum foil and divide the vegetable mixture evenly among them. Fold up the sides of the foil and seal the packets, leaving room for heat to circulate inside. Cook on the grill over high heat, 30 to 35 minutes, until the vegetables are tender. Serve hot.

Serves 4

MAKE IT AT HOME

Preheat the oven to 375°F. Prepare as directed, placing the vegetable mixture in an oiled baking dish. Bake, uncovered, 30 to 35 minutes, until the potatoes are crispy on the outside and tender on the inside. Serve hot.

Potato and Fennel Packets

Any leftovers from this dish are a perfect match with eggs the next morning—leave out the cheese and fry them up like hash browns.

I large red onion, thinly sliced
3/4 pound potatoes, thinly sliced
1½ medium fennel bulbs, thinly sliced
¼ to ½ cup olive oil
I large clove garlic, minced
3 tablespoons Dijon mustard
I teaspoon salt
I teaspoon pepper
Olive oil spray or nonstick cooking spray
6 ounces goat cheese or feta (optional)

Mix the onion, potato, and fennel slices in a large bowl or pot until well combined. Stir in the olive oil, garlic, mustard, salt, and pepper, and toss until well combined.

Spray 4 squares of aluminum foil with olive oil. Divide the vegetable mixture evenly among the squares and wrap into packets, leaving room for heat to circulate inside. Cook on a grill over high heat, 30 to 35 minutes, until the vegetables are tender. Open the packets and crumble cheese over each before serving, if desired.

Serves 4

MAKE IT AT HOME

Preheat the oven to 375°F. Prepare as directed, placing the vegetable mixture in an oiled baking dish. Bake, uncovered, 30 to 35 minutes, until the potato slices are crispy on the outside and tender on the inside. Crumble cheese over before serving, if desired.

Cheesy Biscuits

These crunchy cheese biscuits are perfect for sopping up sauces or just eating by themselves. Use any type of cheese you like. I prefer to use strong cheeses such as sharp cheddar, Gruyère, smoked Gouda, or, for a spicy kick, Monterey Jack with hot peppers. These biscuits are also great with a pat of Spicy Chili Butter (see recipe, page 61), Chipotle-Honey Butter (see recipe, page 62), or Olive Butter (see recipe, page 61).

2 cups (one recipe) Multipurpose Baking Mix (see recipe, page 35)
3/4 cup buttermilk
1/2 cup (1 stick) melted butter, cooled
1 egg, lightly beaten
8 ounces grated cheese (about 1 cup)
Olive oil spray or nonstick cooking spray

Mix all the ingredients (except cooking spray) in a large bowl, using your hands, until a soft, sticky dough forms. Break off a chunk about the size of a golf ball and roll it into a ball between your palms, then flatten it to a patty about 1/2 inch thick and 2 1/2 inches wide. Repeat with the remaining dough.

Spray a skillet with olive oil spray or nonstick cooking spray, or grease with butter. Heat over medium-low heat on the camp stove. When the pan is hot, add the dough patties, pressing them down a bit as you put them in the pan, to make sure that as much of the dough as possible is in contact with the pan. Cook, covered, turning the biscuits over after 4 to 5 minutes or when the bottoms have browned. Replace the lid and continue to cook, about 4 minutes more, until the bottoms are golden brown and the biscuits are cooked through (you may need to split one open to test for doneness). Serve hot.

Makes about 16 small biscuits

MAKE IT AT HOME

Preheat the oven to 375°F. Prepare the dough as directed. Form the dough into 1 large patty, about 1 inch thick. Cut the patty into 8 wedges, and place on a baking sheet. Bake the biscuits, about 20 minutes, until golden brown. Serve warm.

Coconut Couscous

Cooking couscous in coconut milk instead of water gives it an exotic twist.

- 1 14-ounce can light coconut milk (or use 2 parts regular coconut milk diluted with 1 part water)
- 1 cup couscous
- 1 teaspoon salt

Bring the coconut milk to a boil on the camp stove in a saucepan with a lid. Remove from the heat and immediately stir in the couscous and salt. Cover and let stand 5 minutes. Fluff with a fork and serve.

Serves 4

MAKE IT AT HOME

Prepare on the stove top as directed. Serve garnished with Crispy Fried Shallots.

Crispy Fried Shallots

Peel and thinly slice 2 medium shallots. Heat a 2-inch depth of oil in a skillet over medium-high heat until very hot. Carefully drop the shallot slices into the hot oil and cook, stirring, about 2 minutes, until browned. Remove with a slotted spoon, and drain on paper towels until ready to use.

Creamy Polenta

Start with precooked polenta, which is available in tubes at most super-markets. Mix in some milk, butter, and cheese, and you've got yourself a creamy and delicious side dish. It's an ideal accompaniment to Grilled Whole Chicken with Garlic-Herb Butter (see recipe, page 136) or Grilled Eggplant Parmesan (see recipe, page 154) served with Easy Tomato Sauce (see recipe, page 58).

1 cup milk
1 18-ounce tube prepared polenta, diced
1/2 teaspoon salt
2 tablespoons butter
1/2 cup grated Parmesan

Heat, but do not boil, the milk in a large saucepan over medium heat on a camp stove. When the milk is hot, add the polenta chunks, and cook, stirring, until they dissolve, about 5 minutes. Stir in the salt, butter, and cheese. Serve hot.

Serves 4

MAKE IT AT HOME

Regular dry polenta can be baked in the oven for an easy, hands-free side dish.

Preheat the oven to 350°F. Spray an 8-inch-square baking dish with olive oil spray and add 1 cup polenta, 3 1/2 cups water, 1 teaspoon salt, and 2 tablespoons butter. Stir to mix. Bake uncovered for about 50 minutes. Stir in 1/2 cup grated Parmesan and cook another 10 minutes. Spoon onto plates and serve immediately.

CHAPTER 12

DON'T FORGET THE SWEET STUFF: DESSERTS

As much as I love s'mores, even I can only eat so many of them. Following are several recipes for alternatives that won't leave anyone missing that quintessential treat of childhood campouts. Some of these are sure to become new favorites in your camping sweet-treat repertoire.

Baked Chocolate Bananas

S'mores are the ultimate camping dessert, but if you need a break from all that gooey marshmallow, this is a great alternative.

For each serving:
    1 banana
    1 tablespoon semisweet chocolate chips
    1 tablespoon shredded sweetened coconut (optional)

With the banana still in its peel, make an incision lengthwise through the length of the peel and the fruit, leaving the underside of the peel intact. Pull the sides of the banana apart and sprinkle chocolate chips inside. Wrap in aluminum foil and bake over high heat, 10 to 15 minutes, until the fruit is hot and soft and the chocolate is melted. Remove and discard the foil, and sprinkle the coconut over the top, if desired. Serve hot.

Variation:

Omit the chocolate chips and coconut and instead dot the split banana with 1/2 tablespoon of butter cut into small pieces, and sprinkle with 1 tablespoon brown sugar and 1/4 teaspoon ground cinnamon. Proceed with baking according to the recipe above.

Serves 1

MAKE IT AT HOME

Preheat the oven to 400°F. Prepare as directed, baking the foil-wrapped bananas, 10 to 15 minutes, until the fruit is hot and soft and the chocolate is melted. Serve with a scoop of coconut ice cream.

Magic Layer Pie

This stove-top version of the mainstay of childhood bake sales—the "Seven Layer Bar"—may be a bit messier than the original, but it is every bit as delicious. Be sure to allow this dessert to cool completely before serving.

- ¹/₂ stick butter
- 1¹/₂ cups graham cracker crumbs
- 1 cup semisweet chocolate chips
- 1 cup chopped pecans
- 1 cup shredded, sweetened coconut
- 1 14-ounce can sweetened condensed milk

Melt the butter over medium heat in a large skillet on a camp stove. Lower the heat to low, and add the graham cracker crumbs, chocolate chips, pecans, and coconut in layers (in that order), spreading out each ingredient as it is added to form fairly uniform layers. Drizzle the sweetened condensed milk evenly over the top. Cover tightly with a lid or aluminum foil, and cook over low heat, 25 to 30 minutes, until the milk has thickened. Remove from the heat and allow to cool completely. Cut into wedges or squares, and serve.

Serves 6 to 8

MAKE IT AT HOME

Preheat the oven to 350°F. Melt the butter in a 9- by 13-inch baking pan. Continue with the recipe as directed. Bake, about 25 minutes, until golden brown around the edges. Cool on a rack for 15 minutes, cut into squares, and serve.

Maple-Caramel Baked Apples

These apples are very sweet, so half an apple is enough for many people. The recipe is easily doubled for larger servings or more people. I like to serve them atop thick slices of toasted white bread or plain Skillet Scones (see recipe, page 70) to balance out the sweetness.

1/4 cup packed brown sugar
1/4 cup maple syrup
1/2 stick (1/4 cup) butter
2 apples (any type), peeled, cored, and quartered

Mix the brown sugar, maple syrup, and butter in a saucepan over medium heat on a camp stove. Cook, stirring, until the butter is melted and the sauce thickens slightly, 2 to 3 minutes. Be careful not to burn the sauce.

Prepare 4 squares of aluminum foil and place 2 apple quarters on each. Fold up the sides of the foil and drizzle the sauce over the apples, dividing equally among the packets. Wrap the foil securely around the apples, leaving room for heat and steam to circulate inside. Place the packets on a grill over high heat. Cook about 15 minutes, until the apples are tender. Serve in bowls with the sauce from the packet drizzled over the top of the apple quarters.

Serves 4

MAKE IT AT HOME

Preheat the oven to 400°F. Divide the apple pieces among four individual ramekins. Melt the butter, syrup, and sugar together as directed and pour over the apples. Cover the ramekins with foil. Bake, about 15 minutes, until the apples are tender. Serve topped with a scoop of vanilla bean or cinnamon ice cream, or a dollop of whipped cream or crème fraîche.

Rum-Baked Peaches

Nothing signifies the height of summer better than ripe peaches. These peaches baked in foil are as good as any peach pie—and a whole lot easier to make.

> ¹/₂ cup brown sugar
> ¹/₄ cup (¹/₂ stick) butter, cut into small pieces
> 2 tablespoons dark rum
> 4 peaches, peeled, halved, with the pit removed

Mix the sugar and butter together with your hands in a small bowl or pot until the butter is in small clumps. Add the rum and mix until well combined. Place one peach half in the center of a square of foil, dollop one-quarter of the sugar mixture onto it, and top with the other peach half. Repeat with remaining peaches. Wrap the foil tightly around the peaches, and place the packages on the grill over hot coals. Cook, 15 to 20 minutes, until the peaches are soft. Serve hot.

Serves 4

MAKE IT AT HOME

Preheat the oven to 400°F. Prepare the sugar-rum mixture as directed. Place each peach half in a ramekin, dollop one-quarter of the mixture onto each, top with the other peach half, and cover with foil. Bake, about 15 minutes, until the peaches are soft. Serve hot, topped with a scoop of vanilla bean ice cream, or a spoonful of whipped cream or crème fraîche.

S'moradillas

While they'll probably never replace the age-old staple of childhood cookouts, these quesadilla-style s'mores are a lot less messy to eat than the traditional kind—which will please the adults. Though they're great anytime, the kick of cinnamon and the use of tortillas make them an ideal ending for a Mexican dinner.

4 small flour tortillas
$^1/_2$ cup semisweet mini chocolate chips
$^1/_2$ cup mini marshmallows
Cinnamon to taste

Place 2 tortillas on the grill over high heat. Top each with half (about $^1/_4$ cup) the chocolate chips, half (about $^1/_4$ cup) the marshmallows, and a sprinkle of cinnamon. Place the remaining 2 tortillas on top. Cook, 3 to 4 minutes, until the bottom tortilla is lightly browned and crisp. Carefully flip the tortillas. Cook, 3 to 4 minutes more, until the second side is lightly browned and crisp. Cut each into quarters and serve.

Serves 4

MAKE IT AT HOME

Spray a skillet with nonstick cooking spray. Prepare the s'moradillas as directed, and cook over high heat on the stove top as described, about 3 minutes per side, until the tortillas are lightly browned and crisp on both sides. Cut into quarters and serve.

Mexican Hot Chocolate

What could be better for sipping while sitting around the campfire on a cold night?

> 1/2 cup sugar
> 1/4 cup unsweetened cocoa powder
> 1 teaspoon ground cinnamon
> Pinch of salt
> 1/3 cup water
> 4 cups milk
> Marshmallows for garnish (optional)

Mix the sugar, cocoa, cinnamon, and salt in a saucepan on the camp stove until well combined. Stir in the water and bring to a boil over medium heat. Continue cooking about 2 minutes more. Reduce the heat to medium-low and add the milk. Continue to cook (but do not boil), stirring, about 2 minutes more, until the mixture is heated through. Serve hot, garnished with marshmallows if desired.

Serves 4